D0887857

A General Sketch of the
New Testament
in the Light of
Christ and
the Church

WITNESS LEE

PART 1
THE GOSPELS AND THE ACTS

Living Stream Ministry
Anaheim, California • www.lsm.org

First Edition, September 1999.

ISBN 0-7363-0719-2

Published by

Living Stream Ministry
2431 W. La Palma Ave., Anaheim, CA 92801 U.S.A.
P. O. Box 2121, Anaheim, CA 92814 U.S.A.

Printed in the United States of America

99   00   01   02   03   04   /   9   8   7   6   5   4   3   2   1

CONTENTS

PREFACE

This four-part series is composed of messages given by Brother Witness Lee in the summer of 1964. Parts one and two were given in New York City. Parts three and four were given in Los Angeles, California. These messages were not reviewed by the speaker.

CHAPTER ONE

THE SEVEN MAIN ITEMS IN THE GOSPELS

(1)

Scripture Reading: Matt. 1:23; 3:2; 15:30-31; John 6:57; 19:34; 20:22; Acts 2:1-4

If we look carefully into the New Testament with much spiritual insight, we will realize that the twenty-seven books it contains are divided into three groups. The first part consists of five books including the four Gospels and the Acts, which tell us the history of a universal man. The first four books reveal the Head of this universal man—Christ, while the last book in this group shows us His Body. Altogether, these five books give us a full portrait, a full picture, of a universal man.

The second part of the New Testament comprises twenty-one Epistles from Romans through Jude. These twenty-one Epistles are a full description, definition, and explanation of this universal man. The first five books of the New Testament give a portrait, or history, of the universal man but not much definition or explanation. The full definition and explanation of the universal man is found in these twenty-one Epistles.

The last section of the New Testament contains one book, Revelation, which reveals the ultimate consummation of this universal man.

The entire New Testament deals with this universal man. The first group of five books gives us a history of this man, the second group of twenty-one Epistles gives us a full definition of this man, and the last part of the New Testament gives us the consummation of this man. Therefore, the subject of the New Testament is the universal man with his history, his definition, and his consummation. If we keep these four terms in mind—universal man, history, definition, and consummation—we have the entire New Testament. These four key phrases are a great help in understanding the New Testament.

INCARNATION TO MINGLE GOD WITH MAN

In the first four books of the New Testament we first see the Head of this universal man. This Head, Christ, is God the Father in the Son by the Spirit mingling Himself with man and becoming man. Therefore, He is a God-man, God mingled with man, a man who is one with God. Such a wonderful One is the Head of this universal man.

The first matter mentioned in the first chapter of the New Testament is Jesus Christ, who is called Emmanuel (Matt. 1:1, 23). *Emmanuel* means "God with us." This is God with us not only in an objective way but in a very subjective way, not only outside of man but within man. The name Emmanuel was first prophesied by Isaiah (Isa. 7:14). Emmanuel is the name of the child born of a human virgin. This child is called the Mighty God, and although this child is a son, His name is called the Eternal Father (9:6).

By means of chapter one of Matthew, we can see that the significance and importance of Isaiah 7 and 9 are that God Himself came into man to be a little child. The Almighty God came into man to be born of a human virgin (Matt. 1:20, 23) as a little child called Emmanuel, who is God with man and God mingled with man as one. This is the first item mentioned in the New Testament and the first thought in it. In order to understand the New Testament, we must first be impressed with this thought. If we do not have this understanding, we can never get into the real meaning of the New Testament. The beginning of the real meaning of the New Testament is that the Almighty God came into a small man to mingle Himself with man and become a man.

On the first page of the New Testament there is the genealogy of Christ. This genealogy is a very brief sketch of the entire Old Testament. To understand the genealogy in the first chapter of Matthew requires an understanding of the entire Old Testament. All of the names found in this genealogy serve to remind us of the histories and stories of the Old Testament. A new, unlearned believer who reads in Matthew 1:1 that Jesus Christ is the son of Abraham must refer to the first book of the Old Testament in order to find out who Abraham is. In addition, the end of this genealogy also brings us to the end of the Old Testament. In this way, the introduction to the New Testament provides a brief sketch, or review, of the Old Testament. In order to understand the New Testament, we must study the Old Testament and remember the stories in it. It is from this point of view that we can understand the New Testament. No human mind or hand could have written such a record. Only the almighty, wise God could have done this.

The Old Testament types and prophecies point to Christ and the church. In the types and prophecies concerning Christ there are two elements: God and man. The thought of God mingling with man is in the tabernacle, for example. The ark and the boards of the tabernacle were all made of wood overlaid with gold (Exo. 25:10-11; 26:15, 29). Gold typifies God's divine nature, and wood typifies the human nature. This is a picture of Christ, the Head of the universal man.

In the Old Testament types and prophecies we can also see the church as something issuing out of Christ as the wonderful Head, being the same as He is. Because the church is out from Him, it can match Him and be one with Him. Eve as the wife of Adam typifies the church as the wife of Christ, who comes out of Him (Gen. 2:22-23). In the Bible children also typify that the church is exactly the same as Christ in life, nature, and element, because the church is born of God and is out of Him (Isa. 8:18a).

As we have indicated, the first crucial point mentioned in the New Testament is that God Himself came to mingle Himself with man to be a man. This thought is in Matthew 1:18, 20, 23 and Luke 1:35, which speak of Mary conceiving a child by the Holy Spirit, and it is also in John 1, which tells us that the Word, who is God, was incarnated to become a man (vv. 1, 14).

THE KINGDOM FOR THE EXPRESSION
AND AUTHORITY OF GOD

The Kingdom of the Heavens Drawing Near

The first matter in the New Testament is the incarnation, including the birth and growth of Christ. Following this, the second thought, the second matter, revealed is the kingdom. Following the matter of incarnation, the first word proclaimed, announced, and declared in the New Testament is the kingdom. Matthew 3:2 says, "Repent, for the kingdom of the heavens has drawn near." Repentance is necessary because the kingdom is here. The first message of the New Testament gospel is the kingdom. After John the Baptist announced the kingdom, Christ repeated the same thing (4:17), and He instructed His disciples to repeat it again (10:7).

Instead of telling people to repent because the kingdom is here today, Christianity mistakenly asks people to repent in order that they may go to heaven. However, the reason we repent of our sins and receive God's gospel concerning Christ is that the kingdom has drawn near. Our rebirth, our regeneration, is not for going to heaven but for entering into the kingdom of God today (John 3:5). The first word of the New Testament is concerning incarnation, that God became a man as Emmanuel. Then the second word of the New Testament is the kingdom. Through incarnation, Emmanuel brought the kingdom of the heavens to people. Now every human being has to deal with this kingdom.

The Expression of God and the Authority of God

What is the kingdom? Some may answer that it is the rule of the King, but this matter is hard to understand merely by our human mind. The proper definition of the kingdom is found at the close of the prayer that the Lord told us to pray, which says, "Do not bring us into temptation, but deliver us from the evil one. For Yours is the kingdom and the power and the glory forever. Amen" (Matt. 6:13). The word *power* also indicates authority. According to its proper meaning, the kingdom of God is a matter of authority and glory. God's authority is for dealing with His enemy, and God's glory is the very manifestation and expression of God Himself.

This is the reason that two crucial matters are mentioned in the creation of man (Gen. 1:26). The first is that man was created in the image of God for His expression, and the second is that God committed His authority to man for man to rule over all things on this earth, especially over the creeping things. Among the creeping things there is the serpent, which is a symbol of Satan, God's enemy. By reading Genesis chapter one carefully, we can realize that God created man with the authority to rule over the earth, upon which there is the creeping one, the serpent.

Moreover, man was created in the image of God, which is His expression, which equals the glory of God. First Corinthians 11:7a says, "For a man ought not to have his head covered, since he is God's image and glory." Man is the glory of God because he is the image of God; he was made in the image of God for God's expression, that is, for the glory of God. Furthermore, God committed man with His authority to rule over His enemy. This reveals what the kingdom is. On the negative side, the kingdom is for subduing and ruling over God's enemy, while on the positive side, it is to glorify and express God. Hence, God's kingdom is to subdue, conquer, defeat, and overcome all His enemies and also to express His glory.

Incarnation is the mingling of God with man, and along with this incarnation, God's kingdom was brought in to subdue, overcome, conquer, and defeat all His enemies by His divine authority and to express Him in a full way for His glory. We need a heavenly vision of this, not merely a mental understanding.

The Kingdom Coming with the Lord Jesus

While the Lord Jesus was on this earth, the kingdom was here already. When the Pharisees asked Him as to when the kingdom of God should come, He answered them and said, "The kingdom of God does not come with observation; nor will they say, Behold, here it is! or, There! For behold, the kingdom of God is in the midst of you" (Luke 17:20-21). In Matthew 12:28 the Lord also said, "But if I, by the Spirit of

God, cast out the demons, then the kingdom of God has come upon you." Wherever the Lord Jesus went, His enemies were subdued. On the negative side, sin, sickness, demons, evil spirits, and Satan himself were all conquered, subdued, and defeated by Christ. On the positive side, God was expressed and glorified. In His human living on earth, people saw the glory of God, that is, God expressed through Him and in Him. Therefore, wherever He was, there the kingdom was also.

Many people do not have the proper thought concerning the kingdom. It is possible to read the four Gospels by our human mentality and understand them merely in word. However, we need the heavenly vision to have the proper insight. To be sure, we must understand the words, but we must understand them by the heavenly vision. The teaching concerning the kingdom by the Brethren, for example, is too technical, too much in letter, and too dispensational, lacking light and impact. Before God and in the Lord, I have the full assurance to speak the real truth concerning the kingdom, not in doctrine in dead letters but in the way of living revelation. The kingdom is a matter of God's authority and God's glory which was brought to man by His incarnation.

When the Lord Jesus was incarnated as a man to live, walk, and work on this earth, He brought the divine authority and God's glory with Him. Thus, wherever He was, there was God's kingdom. All God's enemies were subdued, conquered, defeated, and overcome, and God's full glory was expressed through Him. This is the full meaning of the kingdom of God. When Christ as the Head comes into us, all the enemies of God within us are also subdued by Him, and the full glory of God is expressed in us. In this way, we have the kingdom of God within us.

The principle will be the same when Christ comes back the second time. On the negative side, Christ will come with the full authority of God to subdue all things. On the positive side, He will express God in a full way as God's glory. This will be the kingdom in its manifestation in full. That is something in the future, but today the same principle is already here. The principle of the kingdom is of two aspects: divine authority to deal with the enemy of God and God's glory to express God Himself.

In order to understand the Scriptures fully, we must first grasp the principles and not the details. In order to understand the map of a big city, for example, we must first know the main streets. If we are clear about the main streets, then we can go anywhere without getting lost or confused. To grasp the main principles and treat the details as secondary is the best way to study any matter. Here, therefore, we are presenting a sketch without getting into many technical details. We must be impressed with the principles. As we have seen, the first principle of the New Testament is incarnation, God mingled with man and becoming a man. The second principle, or main item, of the New Testament is the kingdom. God's divine authority with His full glory was brought to man by His incarnation.

Being Born Again to Enter into the Kingdom

With the kingdom there is a demand, or requirement, which is much higher than the requirements of the Mosaic law (Matt. 5:17-48). The requirements of the law of Moses are that we be just, right, good, kind, and holy, whereas the requirement of the kingdom is that we be the same as God. The Lord Jesus tells us in Matthew 5:48, "You therefore shall be perfect as your heavenly Father is perfect." Not only must we be just, right, good, kind, and holy, but we also must be the same as God. This is the requirement of the kingdom, which far surpasses the requirements of the law.

In order to enter into the kingdom there is a condition. Merely to be good and just is not sufficient. The terms, the condition, for entering the kingdom is that we be born again, that is, born of God (John 3:5; 1:13). Regardless of how good we are, we are still not qualified to enter the kingdom because we need another birth; we must be born anew (3:3). To be born anew means to be born again.

Even if we were as good as Confucius or even better, we still would have no qualifications to enter into the kingdom. No matter how good we are, we must realize that we are only created by God, not born of God. Therefore, in order for us to enter God's kingdom, we must be born of God, that is, we must have the life of God, God Himself within us as life. Merely by our natural life, we can never fulfill the requirements of the kingdom; this is beyond all possibility. We need another life, the divine life, which is God Himself. We must have God Himself within us in order to fulfill the requirements of the kingdom. This is why the opening word of the New Testament tells us to repent for the sake of the kingdom.

The Gospel of the Kingdom

Because we must be born again in order to enter the kingdom, the gospel is called the gospel of the kingdom. We ourselves must preach this gospel of the kingdom (Matt 24:14). The gospel of the kingdom requires human beings to receive God as life to fulfill His kingdom requirements with authority to subdue all God's enemies and with glory to express Him. It is impossible for our natural human life to subdue God's enemies and glorify God in a full way. To do good is the most that our created life can do. If, on the negative side, we are to subdue all God's enemies and, on the positive side, glorify God in a full way, we must have God Himself in us as our life. This is the extract of the teaching of the entire New Testament.

If we consider the four Gospels and the Acts, we will realize that the gospel preached by John the Baptist, by Christ Himself, by the disciples sent by Christ, and by the apostles after the day of Pentecost was the gospel of the kingdom, which brings people into God's kingdom with His authority to overcome all His enemies and express Him in His full glory (Matt. 3:2; 4:17, 23; 9:35; 10:7; Acts 8:12; 19:8). This gospel, which was preached by John the Baptist, by Christ, by the disciples, and by the apostles, must also be announced by us (Matt. 24:14). However, most Christians today preach a low gospel, telling others, "You have no peace or joy, and you will perish in hell, but God loves you and has been merciful to you. Now you must believe in Him to have peace and joy and to go to heaven." This is today's poor, low gospel, a gospel without any glory. However, the gospel preached by John the Baptist, Christ, His disciples, and His apostles was full of glory and authority. It is a gospel of God Himself as our life within for us to subdue, conquer, and overcome all God's enemies and express God in His full glory. This is the gospel of the kingdom, which is the second main item, the second thought, of the New Testament.

THE FALLEN CONDITION OF MAN

The third matter that the New Testament unveils in the four Gospels is the real condition of man. When God was incarnated as a man and brought His kingdom to man, man was in a poor condition. Every case in the four Gospels reveals the condition of man. Man is sinful, full of lusts, sickness, weakness, and death, and he is filled with evil spirits, possessed by demons, and ruled over by Satan in his kingdom of darkness (John 8:7, 11, 21; Matt. 14:14; 15:30-31; Luke 7:12; John 11:11-14; Matt. 8:16; 12:22-28).

Wherever the Lord Jesus went in His ministry on the earth, He encountered sin, sickness, weakness, death, sinful things, demon-possession, evil spirits, and the rule of the darkness of Satan. Furthermore, the condition of mankind is also one of hunger, thirst, dissatisfaction, and disappointment (Matt. 14:14-21; John 7:37). Therefore, the four Gospels show us a full picture, not only of the incarnated God with His kingdom, but of man's fallen condition. Many pages in the four Gospels reveal the real condition of man as the third item, a negative item, of the New Testament.

CHRIST MEETING MAN'S EVERY NEED

The fourth thing that the New Testament reveals to us is that this very Christ meets all of mankind's needs. He is the full answer to all our needs. The first four books of the New Testament testify that whatever man needs, Christ is. If we need life, He is life (John 10:10b). If we need light, He is light (8:12). If we are sick, He is the Healer (Matt. 8:14-16). If we are weak, He is the strength (John 5:8-9). What do you need? If you need redemption, He is also redemption; if you need regeneration, you have it in Christ. Those who were blind came to Him and received sight (Mark 10:46-52; John 9:4-13). The dead were resurrected by Him (John 11:41-44). Those who were sick met Him and were healed (Luke 4:38-40). He filled the hungry ones, satisfied the thirsty ones, and released the demon-possessed ones (John 6:32-35; 7:37; Mark 1:23-28; 5:1-20). There is not one case in these books of a man who had a need that Christ could not meet. Rather, these books show us that Christ is the very answer to all the needs of mankind. This is the fourth item that the New Testament reveals. If we keep these principles in mind when we read the New Testament, we will understand it in a better way.

THE LIVING OF THE DIVINE LIFE
THROUGH THE HUMAN LIFE

The fifth thing that the New Testament shows us is the living of Jesus. Since the beginning of human history, there has never been such a living as the one lived out by this bountiful One, the living of the divine life through a human with the human nature. The daily living, the daily walk, of Jesus was wonderful. On the one hand, such a living conquers all the enemies of God, and on the other hand, it expresses God, manifesting Him in a full way. Thus, this living is the very reality of the kingdom of God.

When we read the four Gospels, we should have a deep impression of the living of this Man, a living of the divine life through a human being. He was a genuine man, yet He lived not by Himself but by God as life (John 6:57). Therefore, He possessed the power and authority to conquer and subdue all of God's enemies. At the same time He was able to express God, manifesting Him in His full glory. Such a living of the bountiful One was the reality of the kingdom of God.

THE IMPARTATION OF GOD'S DIVINE LIFE

The sixth main item revealed in the New Testament is the impartation of God's life by the Lord's death and resurrection (John 19:34; 20:22). By Christ's living of the divine life through the human nature, He conquered the enemies of God and expressed God in full glory. In order for such a life and living to be ours, He had to pass through death and enter into resurrection. By His death and resurrection He imparted

Himself into us as life in order to meet all our needs and fulfill the requirements of the kingdom.

The requirements of the kingdom can be fulfilled only by Christ Himself as life to us. The first three Gospels—Matthew, Mark, and Luke—give us the requirements of the kingdom. The Gospel of John supplies us with the life which fulfills the kingdom's requirements. The kingdom is a matter of requirements, while life is the fulfillment. The first three Gospels show us what the kingdom requires, while the last Gospel tells us how life fulfills the requirements of the kingdom. This life can be ours only through Christ's death and resurrection.

MAN BEING BROUGHT INTO GOD

After the Lord's resurrection, the disciples were filled with the Spirit as breath within (John 20:22), and after His ascension, they were filled with the Spirit as power, as the rushing violent wind without (Acts 2:1-4). The breath is for life, and the rushing wind is for power. At this point, man was brought into God. By incarnation God was brought into man, and by resurrection and ascension man was brought into God. The Lord's coming in incarnation brought God into man, and His going through death, resurrection, and ascension brought man into God. This is the seventh main item revealed in the New Testament.

By His incarnation, Christ brought God from heaven into man on the earth. At that time, there was a man on the earth with God in Him. However, man was not yet in God. Not until Christ died, resurrected, and ascended did Christ bring man into God. Therefore, today in heaven there is a man in God. In incarnation Christ brought God into man on the earth; in His resurrection and ascension He brought man into God in the heavens. What God desired to have was accomplished, for there was then a real mingling of God and man. God is in man and man is in God. God came into man by incarnation, and man is brought into God by Christ's resurrection and ascension.

On this earth there was a man with God in Him, but there had never been a man in the heavens in God until Christ died, resurrected, and ascended. By His incarnation He brought His divine nature into man, and by His resurrection and ascension He brought the human nature into God. Now, God is in man and man is in God. God is in us on the earth, and we are in God in the heavens. We are hidden with Christ in God (Col. 3:3). Through the Son of God, the Father is in us on the earth, and through Christ, we are in God in the heavens.

THE SEVEN MAIN ITEMS IN THE GOSPELS

(2)

Scripture Reading: John 6:57; 7:16-17; 12:49-50; 14:24; 5:17, 19; 10:25; 14:10b; 12:24; 20:17, 22; 19:34; 3:29-30; Col. 3:3

In the previous message we saw the seven main items revealed in the Gospels. These are incarnation, the kingdom with its requirements, the miserable condition of fallen man, the all-sufficiency of Christ to meet man's need, the living of the divine life through and in the human life, Christ's imparting of Himself into man, and man being brought into God through Christ's death, resurrection, and ascension.

We must know these seven items as thoroughly as we know God's redemption. We respect God's redemption in Christ very much. However, today in Christianity people are clear concerning Christ's redemption, but they are not clear, for example, about Christ's imparting Himself into us. These seven points are the very essence of the four Gospels. Unless we grasp these seven points and have a proper impression of them, we cannot understand the depth and real meaning of the Gospels; we will understand the Gospels in a very superficial way. On the surface, it may seem that we understand them, but we will not understand them deeply if we do not have this insight.

INCARNATION—THE MINGLING OF DIVINITY
WITH HUMANITY

The books which comprise the first part of the New Testament first reveal that God has mingled Himself with man and has become a man, putting man on Himself to live with man and as man. We can never exhaust the consideration, understanding, and realization of this point. We must all grasp, realize, and consider this matter more and more. One day the eternal, infinite, unlimited God, who is the almighty Creator, came into man and mingled Himself with man as one in order to live in man and live as a man. This is truly wonderful!

The general teaching in Christianity concerning the incarnation is that God's Son had to become a man in order to save man. However, this is too shallow and superficial. We may have never heard that incarnation is the mingling of divinity with humanity. God's intention is to mingle Himself with man. Divinity must be one with humanity. This is not merely for the purpose of saving man. Even if man had never fallen, divinity would still need to be mingled with humanity. This was God's original plan and heart's desire. God desires to mingle Himself with man. This is His delight. Therefore, one day He came into man and became a man. He lived with man, in man, and as a man. He spoke, walked, talked, and did things as a man.

CHRIST BRINGING THE KINGDOM TO MAN

Second, when Christ came to man in this way, He brought with Him the kingdom. Without the kingdom there is no possibility for God to accomplish His purpose. A man's home may be considered his kingdom. He is the "king," and his wife and children are his "subjects." This is to work out what is on his heart, to accomplish his plan. A kingdom is a sphere, a realm, in which we exercise authority to do things and work out what is in our heart.

The only way for God to accomplish His desire is by having a kingdom. He must have a sphere, a realm, in which He can reign. In this way He can exercise and manifest His authority to rule over things and accomplish what is on His heart. When Christ was incarnated, His kingdom was brought to man. Hence, the kingdom with its requirements is emphasized strongly in the New Testament.

THE MISERABLE CONDITION OF FALLEN MAN

The third main item revealed in the first section of the

New Testament is the miserable condition of fallen man. In the four Gospels many cases are mentioned which show us the real condition of fallen man. Man is sinful, weak, full of sickness and death, possessed by demons, taken over by evil spirits and by darkness, and under the power and in the kingdom of the evil one. Wherever this incarnated One went, He encountered these things.

CHRIST'S SUFFICIENCY IN MEETING MAN'S NEED

In addition, all these cases reveal to us the all-sufficiency of Christ in meeting man's need. There was not one case in which Christ could not meet the need. The four Gospels give us a record of man's condition and Christ's sufficiency to meet man's need.

The first two items above—the incarnation and the kingdom—are very important, but they are neglected by many Christians today. The third and fourth items, however, are not as important as the first two, but they are overemphasized by many today. Wherever we go, we may hear people speaking about the miserable condition of fallen man and the sufficiency of Christ to meet our need. This shows us that people often take secondary matters as being primary.

THE LIVING OF THE DIVINE LIFE
THROUGH THE HUMAN LIFE

The fifth, sixth, and seventh of the main items of the New Testament are especially deep and vitally important. The fifth item is the wonderful living of the Lord Jesus, a living which was not a human life alone but a living of the divine life through the human life.

Four Kinds of Life

According to Genesis 1 and 2, in the entire universe there are four different kinds of life. The first is the vegetable life, the lowest life without consciousness. The second is the animal life, the lower life with consciousness. The third is the human life, the higher life with consciousness. The fourth is the highest life in the universe—the uncreated, eternal, divine life which is God Himself. The first three kinds of life are found in Genesis 1, while the last kind is found in Genesis 2:9. This, of course, does not include the angelic life, which is not mentioned in Genesis 1 and 2. The angels were created as part of God's original creation, but Genesis 1:2 through the end of chapter two is not the record of God's original creation but an account of the recovery of God's creation.

In the entire history of the human race and of the universe itself, there had never been a living which was the living out of the divine life. There had been the living of the vegetable life, the animal life, and the human life, but there had never been the living out of the divine life in the human life, a living which is a combination of the divine life with the human life as God Himself living in man and through man.

The Genuine Christian Living

Such a living is very wonderful, and it must be our Christian living. What is the Christian living? The Christian living is the divine life, God Himself, lived out of humanity. This must be our Christian living today. Our Christian living must be the living out of God Himself through man, a living by the divine life through the human life. In the record of the four Gospels, especially the Gospel of John, there was a man on the earth who lived not by His own life but by another life (John 6:57). He was a man, but He always lived by God, by the divine life. He was a man with the living of God. He had a wonderful living, which was a combination of God's life with the human life.

From my youth I heard many Christian teachers and ministers speaking about love. They told us that Christianity is the religion of love, so we should love others. We were instructed from the Scriptures to love our neighbors, to love one another, and to love even our enemies. However, even if all Christians could love others, that is not the real Christian love. Genuine Christian love is not from ourselves; it is a love by God, by the divine life. We may love others by ourselves, but that is not genuine Christian love. It is not a matter of our own love but a matter of living out God. We must live out God and live God through us. The genuine Christian living is not a matter of loving or hating, or of being humble or proud; it is a matter of living out God.

The Living of the Lord Jesus

The principle of the New Testament is that man would not live by the human life but by the divine life. The living that the Lord Jesus had while He was on earth was the living of the divine life mingled with the human life. Although this wonderful Jesus had His human life, He did not live by that human life; rather, He lived by God as His life. When this man spoke, He did not speak by His own life but by God's life (John 7:16-17; 12:49-50; 14:24). When this man worked, He did not work by His own life but by God as His life (5:17, 19; 10:25; 14:10b). The first few books of the New Testament reveal a wonderful, real man living on this earth not by His own life but by God as His life. This is the living of Jesus, which is the fifth main item mentioned in the four Gospels.

The entire Gospel of Matthew shows us that with the living of Jesus there was the kingdom of God and the real submission to God. The kingdom of God was brought in to exercise God's authority because there was a person who was completely submissive to God's authority.

The Gospel of Mark shows us the living of Jesus as one who was fully obedient to God.

The Gospel of Luke shows us the living of a very proper, normal man. Such a man was absolutely separated, holy, toward God; He was righteous with Himself, being wrong with others in no way; and He was always peaceful, kind, and good toward others.

In the Gospel of John we see the living of Jesus as the living of a human life mingled with the divine life. Man and God, God and man, are mingled together to live, to walk, and to work as one.

In summary, the Gospel of Matthew shows us a living which brings in the exercise of God's authority and causes people to submit to His authority in a full way. In the Gospel of Mark we find a person who lives a life in absolute obedience to God to serve God's will and His purpose. Luke's Gospel presents the Lord Jesus as a proper, normal person who is wrong in no way with God, with Himself, and with others. Jesus could be such a perfect man because He had this kind of living. The Gospel of John shows us a human life mingled with the divine life. These two lives live, walk, work, think, and do things together. In everything, these two lives are one.

THE MASS REPRODUCTION OF THE GOD-MAN

Such a wonderful God-man, a man with God living in Him, needs to be duplicated and reproduced. This is the sixth major item in the New Testament. For this purpose, He needs to impart Himself into many others. In this way, Christ may be likened to a stencil for copying. Everything of the Lord is composed as a stencil in order to be duplicated and reproduced. Such a man with such a wonderful life and living must be duplicated in the way of mass reproduction.

One Grain Becoming Many Grains

This man with such a living is likened to a grain of wheat that is multiplied (John 12:24). The way in which this grain of wheat is multiplied is by death and resurrection. By His death and resurrection, Christ imparted Himself into all His believers (20:22; 1 Pet. 1:3). The one grain of wheat after death and resurrection became many grains. This is the imparting of Christ into us. At the beginning of the four Gospels Christ was the only begotten Son of God (John 3:18), the one grain of wheat, but at the end of the Gospels Christ became the Firstborn among many brothers (20:17), the first of many grains. The one grain became many grains because He imparted Himself into many others.

Redemption and Life-imparting

The Lord's death and resurrection are a matter not only of Christ imparting Himself to us but also of His redemption. By His death Christ redeemed and recovered us, bringing us back to God. However, redemption is not all; redemption is for imparting life, just as cleaning a cup is for the purpose of filling it. In order to use a cup in the way we intend, we must clean it; then after cleaning it, we can fill it. Christ's work is in this principle. After He redeemed us, He fills us with Himself as life. In this way, redemption and life-imparting always go together.

John 19:34 says, "One of the soldiers pierced His side with a spear, and immediately there came out blood and water." Two things flowed out of the Lord's side: blood and water. The blood is mentioned first and then the water. The blood is for redeeming and cleansing, and the water signifies the imparting, the life-giving, of Christ. In this verse, redemption comes first and life-imparting is second, just as we must clean a cup before we can fill it. This is because John 19 shows us the process of redemption and filling. Redemption, however, is supplementary to God's goal; it is not the original goal. In the process, Christ needed to redeem us before He could fill us, but God's original goal is that man would be filled with His life.

At the Lord's table there are also two items: the bread and the cup. The bread is of fine flour from wheat, and the cup is of wine. The cup represents the redeeming blood of Christ, and the bread speaks of the imparting of Christ Himself. Of these two items, the bread is the goal, and the cup is a supplementary item. Because of the accomplishing of Christ's process, we can testify at the Lord's table that we are one with the Lord; this is signified by the bread, which comes first. Our testimony is our oneness with Him, as seen in the bread, the loaf, the body of Christ. Following this, we declare to the universe that we, the fallen race, can be one with the Lord because of His redemption. As fallen, sinful, dirty, evil people, we can be one with the holy One by His blood. The cup, therefore, is supplementary to the main item, the main testimony, which is the bread. Although we were sinful, dirty, and fallen, we are one with Him and one in Him because He has shed His blood for us. Therefore, at the Lord's table we first partake of the bread and then we share the cup.

We must always keep in mind that in the Lord's death and resurrection there is redemption and the impartation of Christ. In John 19 redemption is signified first, but this is not the most important thing; it is part of the process as an additional matter. The foremost matter is the life-imparting aspect that enables us to be one with Him. The imparting of life always requires redemption. Without Christ's redemption, it is impossible for Him to impart His life into us. Similarly, without cleansing it is impossible for a cup to be filled up; the filling of a cup includes its cleansing. Therefore, the imparting, the life-giving, of Christ includes His redemption. It is by redemption and life-imparting that the created and fallen man is made one with God.

The Increase of Christ

In John 3:29-30 John the Baptist said, "He who has the bride is the bridegroom; but the friend of the bridegroom, who stands and hears him, rejoices with joy because of the bridegroom's voice. This joy of mine therefore is made full. He must increase, but I must decrease." The bride here is the increase of Christ just as Eve, the wife of Adam, was the increase of Adam. Originally, God did not create a man and a woman at the same time. God created only a single man, a bachelor. However, God said that it was not good for the man to be alone (Gen. 2:18). Man needed an increase, a counterpart to match him. God took a rib out of Adam, and that part became Eve, his counterpart, his increase (v. 22). After that, if we were to look at Adam, we would see not Adam alone but Adam with a wife as his increase. Before His death and resurrection Christ was single; He was alone. In His resurrection He gained His increase as the bride to match Him.

John 12:24 tells us that the one grain of wheat fell into the earth and died to produce many grains as the increase of Christ. Chapter fifteen of the same Gospel speaks of the many branches which are the increase of the vine (vv. 1-5). In John 17 the Lord prayed that all of His believers might be one (v. 21). The many grains are crushed and ground into fine flour to be blended together as one loaf, one Body. This indicates that the oneness mentioned in the Lord's prayer in John 17 is for the Body. All the believers of Christ must be one, and this oneness is for the Body. In addition, in 20:17 the Lord spoke of "My brothers." After His resurrection, He told Mary to go to His brothers, who are the reproduction, the duplication, of Himself. The many brothers are blended and built together to become one Body signified by the bread. This is the duplication, the reproduction, of Christ.

MAN BROUGHT INTO GOD

The last important point revealed in the four Gospels is that man is brought into God. By His incarnation, God was brought into man; God was made one with man. Now by Christ's redemption and life-imparting, man is made one with God. God is now one with man, and man is one with God. Not only we are human but Christ also has the human nature. He is God in man and man in God. In this way, God has accomplished His work. He brought God into man to make God one with man, and He also brought man into God to make this man one with God. Now man and God, God and man, are one.

Therefore, it is not easy to say where we are. While we are on this earth, we are also in the heavenly places. This is why Colossians 3:3 tells us that our life has been hidden with Christ in God. We are in the heavenlies because we are one with God. At the same time God is in us on the earth. We may illustrate this with electric lamps. Without electricity the lamps are separated from the electric generator and from one another. In the electricity, however, all the lamps are one with the generator, and the generator is one with the lamps. By Christ's incarnation God has been brought into man, and by His redemption and life-imparting, man has been brought into God. Now God and man, man and God, are one. This is the meaning of our being in Christ and our abiding in Him.

These are truly high and wonderful matters. We must realize Christ's work to the extent that we are clear about these truths, which are mostly neglected by Christianity today. May the Lord reveal these truths to us! May He remove the veils from our eyes and grant us this vision!

The above points are the depth of the meaning of the four Gospels. By His incarnation, Christ brought God into man, and with Him there was the kingdom of God. Then, by His redemption and life-imparting, He brought man into God; He made us one with God. Now we are not merely men but God-men, men mingled with God. We are one with Him and one with one another. Therefore, He is the Head and we are the Body. Hence, we can now live a life exactly as He lived on this earth. This is the depth of the real meaning of the four Gospels. If we read the four Gospels from this point of view, we will be able to understand them more deeply.

CHAPTER THREE

THE SIGNIFICANT ITEMS
OF THE NEW TESTAMENT AND
THE PROPHECIES OF THE OLD TESTAMENT

Scripture Reading: John 1:14; 6:57a; Eph. 1:22-23; John 3:29; Rev. 21:9-10; Gen. 3:15; 22:18; Isa. 11:1, 10; 7:14; 9:6; 53:2; Micah 5:2; Gen. 2:21-24; Psa. 22:22; Isa. 8:18

The focus of these messages is a general sketch of the New Testament in the light of Christ and the church. Here we cannot deal with many details, but by the grace of the Lord, we will see the main points and the main line of the New Testament.

In order to know the sketch of the New Testament, we must see something concerning the entire Scriptures. First, the entire Scriptures reveal not only the nature and character of God but also His purpose. In fact, the Scriptures may reveal God's purpose more than His character and nature because the entire Bible is a book showing us God's plan; it is a book unveiling the purpose of God. What is the purpose of God? In brief, God's eternal purpose and intention are to have a group of living persons mingled with Himself as one to be His living, corporate expression.

Second, the Old Testament, the first main part of the Scriptures, contains types and prophecies as figures, shadows, and predictions concerning the purpose of God. In the Old Testament are all the figures, shadows, and pictures which describe, portray, or predict God's eternal purpose.

Third, the New Testament contains the fulfillment of the types and prophecies concerning God's eternal purpose. By this brief and clear word we can see that the entire Scriptures are a book of God's purpose: The Old Testament contains the shadows and figures of God's purpose, and the New Testament contains the fulfillment of His purpose. With this understanding and realization, we can better understand the New Testament.

THE SIGNIFICANT ITEMS OF THE NEW TESTAMENT

Incarnation

To grasp a few significant items is sufficient for us to understand the entire New Testament. The first significant and prominent item mentioned and recorded in the New Testament is that one day God came into man to be mingled with man and to become a man. The almighty Creator of the universe came into one of His creatures, man. This is wonderful! Before incarnation, God was God and man was man; the Creator was the Creator, the creature was the creature, and the two were not one. Incarnation, however, is a real landmark in time, dividing the dispensation of the Old Testament from that of the New Testament. It is a landmark at which something wonderful, magnificent, marvelous, and indescribable happened: The Creator mingled Himself with one of His creatures—man—and He Himself became a man.

A Wonderful Life and Living

Second, the New Testament shows us a wonderful living, a walk as the expression of an inner life. On this earth the Lord Jesus had the living of the divine life through the human life. The wonderful living of the Lord Jesus spoken of and recorded in the four Gospels was the issue of the mingling of the divine life with the human life. In other words, God was lived out through man in a wonderful living. In this living we can see God expressed through man and God and man mingled as one. If we read the four Gospels again with this light and from this point of view, we will have a new understanding of the record of these four books. They show us the wonderful living of God Himself through man and among men.

The Universal Man

The third great matter that the New Testament reveals is

a universal man, a man so great as to fill the entire universe (Eph. 1:23). This man, being universally full without limitation, is in the heavens and on the earth at the same time. The Head of this universal man is Christ, and the Body is the church composed of millions of believers as His members (v. 22). The entire New Testament record is a portrait of such a universal man.

The Bridegroom and the Bride

The entire New Testament also reveals a couple composed of Christ as the Bridegroom and the church as the bride. A couple is two persons who have become one. In John 3:29, John the Baptist told us clearly that Christ came as the Bridegroom for the bride. God became a man to be the Bridegroom to marry a bride. This is why there is a wedding at the end of the New Testament. At the close of the New Testament there is a marriage (Rev. 19:7; 22:17), and before the wedding there is a period of time for the preparation of the bride. The Bridegroom has been waiting for the bride to be ready. When the bride makes herself ready, then the wedding day will come. At the end of the New Testament there is the New Jerusalem which is the bride of Christ (21:9-10). The New Jerusalem is the bride, and Christ as the Lamb of God is the Bridegroom. These two are the universal couple.

The New Jerusalem

Lastly the New Testament shows us the New Jerusalem as the ultimate consummation of God's work in the universe. The New Jerusalem is the ultimate consummation of the church and of all God's work through all the generations. It is also the consummation of the whole universe. Without the New Jersalem as the ultimate sign of God's consummated work, we could never understand the real purpose of His work through the generations. Because this ultimate consummation is recorded and revealed in the New Testament, we know the purpose of God's work, and we have a full description and definition of the purpose and meaning of the entire universe.

THE PROPHECIES OF THE OLD TESTAMENT

The Central Thought of All Prophecies Being Christ and the Church

In order to understand the New Testament we must also examine the prophecies of the Old Testament. In my early years I studied many books on prophecy, including several by G. H. Pember: *The Great Prophecies of the Centuries concerning Israel and the Gentiles, The Great Prophecies concerning the Gentiles, the Jews, and the Church of God,* and *The Great Prophecies of the Centuries concerning the Church.* Mr. Pember gave people much help in understanding the prophecy of the Scriptures. All Bible students agree that Mr. Pember was a real scholar. However, Pember's interpretations of prophecy reveal much about events but not much concerning the central thought of God. The central thought of prophecy is not the events mentioned in the prophecies; rather, it is Christ and the church. Mr. Pember's interpretation of prophecy mainly tells us what will happen to the nation of Israel, to the church, and to the Gentile world. However, the two central matters of the prophecies of the Old Testament are Christ and the church. At this time we cannot go into the details of all the prophecies in the Old Testament. We will point out only a few of the main items.

Old Testament Prophecies concerning Christ

The Seed of Woman

The first prophecy concerning Christ in the Old Testament is the seed of the woman, which is found in Genesis 3:15. Neither Adam nor any of his direct descendants were this seed of woman. Christ is the unique seed of the woman. He is the only one among the entire human race that was born only of a woman. Apparently, we are all born of our mother, but in actuality we are born of our father. Someone may say that Cain, for example, was the son of Adam and of Eve, but the Scriptures do not say this. Rather, Cain and Abel were both the sons of Adam. All human beings are the sons of Adam, the descendants of a man. Among the entire human race, there is only one person of human blood and flesh whose birth had nothing to do with a man.

The fulfillment of this prophecy in the New Testament is found in Galatians 4:4 which says, "When the fullness of the time came, God sent forth His Son, born of a woman, born under law." Similarly, Matthew 1:23 says, "Behold, the virgin shall be with child and shall bear a son."

The Seed of Abraham

Genesis 22:18 records the second main prophecy concerning Christ. In this verse Christ is prophesied as the seed of Abraham. This prophecy was repeated to Isaac in Genesis 26:4 and again to Jacob in Genesis 28:14. These three verses are not three prophecies but one prophecy of Christ as the seed of Abraham. The fulfillment of this prophetic word is in Galatians 3:16; it is also in Matthew 1:1, which says that Christ is the Son of Abraham.

The Seed of David

The third prophecy concerns Christ as the seed of David. Christ as the seed of David is predicted in 2 Samuel 7:12-14 and Isaiah 11:1-5 and 10. Isaiah 11:1 says, "Then a sprout will come forth from the stump of Jesse, / And a branch from his roots will bear fruit." By reading verses 1 through 5, we can realize that this branch is Christ, who comes out of Jesse as the root.

The first verse in the New Testament, Matthew 1:1, is very meaningful, telling us that Christ is the son not only of Abraham but also of David. Jesse was the father of David, and David was the forefather of Christ. Therefore, Jesse also is the forefather of Christ. From this point of view, Christ is the branch coming out of the root, the descendant coming out of the forefather. Isaiah 11:10, however, speaks of Christ as the root of Jesse. In this verse, Christ is no longer the descendant of Jesse but his root. Revelation 5:5 refers to Christ as "the Lion of the tribe of Judah, the Root of David." As the Root of David, Christ is David's forefather, but as the branch, Christ is David's descendant.

In Matthew 22:41-46 Christ questioned the Pharisees in

His wisdom. These verses say, "Now while the Pharisees were gathered together, Jesus questioned them, saying, What do you think concerning the Christ? Whose son is He? They said to Him, David's. He said to them, How then does David in spirit call Him Lord, saying, 'The Lord said to my Lord, Sit at My right hand until I put Your enemies underneath Your feet'? If then David calls Him Lord, how is He his son? And no one was able to answer Him a word, nor did anyone from that day dare to question Him anymore." On the one hand, Christ is the Son of David who came out of David, while on the other hand, He is the Lord of David, the Root of David out of whom David came. Christ is the wonderful One who is everything: He is the root, the branch, and the sprout. He is the Son, yet He is the source.

The central thought of all of these prophecies is that God wants to mingle Himself with man. Therefore, on the one hand, Christ is man, but on the other hand, He is God. As a man He is the sprout, the branch, while as God He is the root, the source. The central message of the prophecies of the Old Testament is that God Himself mingles with man to be a man. Because Christ is both God and man, He is both the branch and the root. As man He is the expression; as God He is the source. Such a Christ is the wonderful One. If we do not know this One, our mouth will be shut like the mouths of the Pharisees (v. 46), and we will not be able to understand the Scriptures.

Immanuel

The fourth great prophecy concerns Christ as Immanuel (Isa. 7:14). The name Immanuel means "God with us." This prophecy is all-inclusive because a son born of a virgin includes the thought of the seed of woman, the seed of Abraham, and the seed of David. The seed of woman, who is also the seed of Abraham and the seed of David, is Immanuel. The central thought of the prophecy concerning Immanuel is that God is with man. Even in the very name of Immanuel there is both God and man. In Hebrew the last two letters of Immanuel—*el*—mean God, and "with us" indicates man. Therefore, in this one name there is the mingling of God with man.

The New Testament fulfillment of this prophecy is found in Matthew 1. Chapter one of Matthew is very profound. In this chapter the above four prophecies are fulfilled: the seed of woman as the son born of a virgin (v. 23), the seed (son) of Abraham (v. 1b), the seed (son) of David (v. 1a), and Emmanuel (v. 23). Such a One is God mingled with man.

The Child as the Mighty God and the Son as the Eternal Father

Isaiah 9:6 records the fifth main prophecy concerning Christ. This verse says, "For a child is born to us, / A son is given to us; / And the government / Is upon His shoulder; / And His name will be called / Wonderful Counselor, / Mighty God, / Eternal Father, / Prince of Peace." The little child born in a manger in Bethlehem is called Mighty God, and the son who is given to us is called Eternal Father. Again, this prophecy shows us the mingling of God with man and the oneness of the expression with the source. Man is the expression, and God is the source; the Son is the expression, and the Father is the source. However, these two are not separate but are mingled as one. The expression is one hundred percent in oneness with the source, as indicated by the fact that the Son is called the Father. The central thought of God, that He mingles Himself with man, is clearly seen in Isaiah 9:6 in that the expression is one with the source.

A Root Out of Dry Ground

Another major prophecy concerns Christ as a root out of dry ground (Isa. 53:2). Here Christ is prophesied not as the eternal root mentioned in Isaiah 11 but as a root in time. Christ as the eternal root is God Himself as the Lord and Creator, yet here He is another root, a root in time, grown out of dry ground. The root out of dry ground refers to the human life and living of the Lord Jesus. As the root in time, He grew up in a poor family, in a poor home, and in a small city (John 1:45-46). He was truly out of dry ground; there was nothing rich in His living.

The great thought hidden within this prophecy concerning Christ, as well as in all the above prophecies, is that this wonderful One is the mingling of God with man. Christ is the eternal root because He is the very Creator, the eternal God, and He is also the root out of dry ground because He became a man to grow up on this earth in a poor situation and poor environment. Christ is God and He is man.

The Eternal One

Christ is also prophesied as the eternal One in Micah 5:2. This verse says, "But you, O Bethlehem Ephrathah, / So little to be among the thousands of Judah, / From you there will come forth to Me / He who is to be Ruler in Israel; / And His goings forth are from ancient times, / From the days of eternity." On the one hand, this short verse tells us that this Ruler of Israel came out of Judah, that is, out of the human source, but on the other hand, it tells us that He came out of eternity. The fact that He came first out of eternity and then out of Judah means that He is God becoming a man. If we lack the vision, we will acknowledge Him as only a Jew. However, He is more than a Jew; He came not only out of the Jewish race but also out of eternity. Hence, He is God becoming a man as the mingling of God with man.

Moreover, Psalm 102:26-27 tells us that Christ is eternal not only in the past but also in the future. According to Micah 5:2, Christ is eternal in the past, and according to Psalm 102, He is eternal in the future. Therefore, He is eternally without beginning and without end. Hebrews 7:3 is the fulfillment of this prophecy. This verse says, "Without father, without mother, without genealogy; having neither beginning of days nor end of life." This wonderful One has no beginning and no end.

In conclusion, the seven main points above are all prophecies concerning this wonderful Christ. Christ is the seed of the woman, the seed of Abraham, and the seed of David who is called Immanuel. This Immanuel is a child who is called Mighty God, and He is a son called Eternal Father. He is also a root out of dry ground. He has no beginning from eternity past, and He has no end unto eternity future. This wonderful One is the mingling of God with man.

I have read many books about the prophecies in the Old

Testament, but almost none present them according to their central thought. The central thought of the prophecies is that God became a man; He was born of a virgin to be a little child and to grow up out of dry ground, yet He is the very God. He is the branch, and He is the root. He is a man of God and God in man. He is everything! This is the wonderful One who was God coming into man, becoming a man, to mingle Himself with man as everything. Christ is a child, yet this child is called Mighty God. He is also a son, yet this Son is called Eternal Father. He came out of the Jewish race, yet He is from eternity. He is the Son of David, yet He is the Lord of David. He is the branch, yet He is the root.

The entire Old Testament is centered around the mingling of God and man. If we grasp the central thought of all the prophecies, they will be clear to us. If, however, we miss the central thought, we can never understand the Scriptures. The Scriptures reveal the thought that man is mingled with God. God Himself is the very life, the very content, and man is the expression. Man expresses God's life within him as his content.

Old Testament Types of the Church

The central thought of all the prophecies is realized first in Christ and then in the church. In Christ we see God mingled with man, and in the church we also see God mingled with man.

Eve Coming Out of Adam

The first prophecy of the church is in the form of a type, which is the record of Eve in Genesis 2:21-24. As the wife of Adam, Eve is a type of the church. Eve came out of Adam to be the counterpart of Adam, to match Adam. This is a type of the church, showing us how the church comes into existence and what the function of the church is. This type is fulfilled in Ephesians 5:31-32.

The Many Brothers of the Firstborn

A second great prophecy of the church is in Psalm 22:22. This verse, speaking of the resurrection of Christ, says, "I will declare Your name to my brothers; / In the midst of the assembly I will praise You." The fulfillment of this type is in John 20 and Hebrews 2. John 20:17 says that after His resurrection, the Lord Jesus called His disciples "My brothers," and Hebrews 2:12 tells us that these brothers are the church. The church is a composition, the assembly, of the many brothers of Christ the firstborn Son.

The Children of the Father

A third major Old Testament prophecy of the church is that of the children of the Father. This is found in Isaiah 8:18, which says, "See, I and the children whom Jehovah has given me." In this verse the "I" is Christ, and the children are the members of the church. This prophecy is fulfilled in Hebrews 2:13.

The above are the main prophecies of the church found in the Old Testament. In summary, the church is the same to Christ as Eve was to Adam; that is, the church comes out of Christ to match Christ and be one with Christ. The church is also the many brothers of the Firstborn having the same life and nature as Christ. Christ is the Firstborn, and the church is composed of His many brothers. Third, the church comprises the children whom the Father gave to Christ. The church issues from Christ as life because all of the members of the church are born of Christ, who is the very source of the church.

The above prophecies emphasize that Christ is the mingling of God with man, and the church is the counterpart of Christ, the many brothers with Christ the Firstborn, and the children given to Christ. These three prophecies clearly show us that the church is a part of Christ, born of Christ to match Him, and one with Christ. This is the central thought of the prophecies in the Old Testament concerning Christ and the church and their fulfillment in the New Testament.

CHAPTER FOUR

THE SEVEN MAIN ITEMS IN THE GOSPELS

(3)

In this chapter we will once again review the general subject of the entire New Testament. As we saw in the previous chapters, we may express this subject in four terms: a universal man with Christ as the Head and the church as His Body, the history of this universal man, the definition and explanation of the universal man, and the consummation of the universal man. These four items give us a full picture of the New Testament in detail. In addition, we saw that the Old Testament is composed mainly of types and prophecies. Two central matters, Christ and the church, are the fulfillment of all the types and prophecies of the Old Testament.

THE SIGNIFICANCE OF THE PROPHECIES CONCERNING CHRIST AND THE CHURCH

Christ Prophesied in Persons, Times, and Places

The real significance of the prophecies concerning Christ is the mingling of God and man. This divine One, Christ, intends to mingle Himself with man. This is the proper insight into the persons, times, and places in all the prophecies. Related to the Lord's person, for example, Christ is called Immanuel (Isa. 7:14). In this one wonderful name, there is God and man, a man filled with God. Isaiah 9:6 also tells us that a child is born, yet His name is called Mighty God, and a son is given, yet His name is called Eternal Father. All of these names related to persons show us this wonderful One who is God Himself mingled with man.

Then, in the matter of time, Christ came forth in time, yet

His goings forth are from ancient times, from the days of eternity (Micah 5:2). His goings forth are from eternity, yet His appearing is in time. Here again is the principle of mingling. Only God Himself is in eternity, and the creatures of God are in time. The eternal Creator had the intention to mingle Himself with His creatures in time.

Related to places, Christ came out of Judea, yet He came from an eternal place. All of these Old Testament prophecies give us a picture of God's intention to mingle Himself with the human race. This insight into the real meaning of prophecies has been nearly lost in Christianity. Many Christian teachers speak about these prophecies, but they do not grasp the central insight into them. The central insight into the prophecies is that God's intention is to come into man and mingle Himself with man.

The Church as the Bride, the Brothers, and the Children

The Old Testament prophecies also speak concerning the church. The type of Adam and Eve signifies that the church as the bride of Christ is a part of Christ (Gen. 2:22-24; Eph. 5:31-32). A wife is the counterpart of the husband, and the husband and wife joined together are a perfect whole. If we have the spiritual insight, we can realize that a man or woman alone is only one half. A woman must match a man by marrying him; then the two will be one whole. We may illustrate a man and a woman by a watermelon. If we cut a watermelon in half, there are two parts, each having a round side and a flat side. If we match the two flat sides together, the melon is whole. In the same way, the husband is a part to the wife, and the wife is a counterpart to the husband. The two must match each other to make a perfect whole. A whole man is not a man alone; it is a man with his counterpart, his wife. This reveals a deep truth in the Bible.

In numbering people, both the Old Testament and the New Testament often do not reckon the females (Num. 1:2; John 6:10). This is because the female is the counterpart of the male. Through all the generations and around the globe, a bride always covers her head during the wedding. In every kind of wedding, whether in China, Indonesia, or India, the bride's head is covered. In this way, at a wedding there are two persons but only one head. When the bride marries a bridegroom, she takes him as her head and covers her own head. Then from the wedding day on, these two become one. This is a picture of the church's relationship to Christ. The church is Christ's counterpart to match Christ, to be a part of Christ. For this reason, Ephesians 5:31 says, "A man shall leave his father and mother and shall be joined to his wife, and the two shall be one flesh." This means that the church is a part of Christ.

The church is also revealed as the many brothers of Christ as His multiplication (Psa. 22:22; John 20:17; Heb. 2:11-12). Originally Christ was the only begotten Son of God (John 1:18), but in resurrection He became the Firstborn among many brothers (Rom. 8:29). The one grain became many grains (John 12:24) as the duplication and multiplication of the one grain. In this way, the church is the multiplication of Christ.

Furthermore, the church is prophesied as the many children given to Christ (Isa. 8:18; Heb. 2:13). The church has the same life and nature as Christ. Christ is the very source of the church, and the church is born of this source.

In summary, the church as the bride of Christ is a part of Christ, the church as the many brothers of Christ is Christ's multiplication and duplication, and the church as the children given to Christ has the same life and nature as Christ. This insight into the church helps us to thoroughly understand what the church is. We do not need to say much; just by these three aspects we can have a clear understanding of the church. What is the church? The church is a part of Christ and the multiplication of Christ, having the same life and nature as Christ.

THE SEVEN MAJOR POINTS IN THE FOUR GOSPELS

Incarnation

When we come to the first four books of the New Testament, we can see seven major points. The first item that the

New Testament shows us is incarnation. The entire Old Testament leads us to the point that God is brought into man. God coming to be a man and mingling Himself with man is the first item of the New Testament. If we have this insight, the entire holy Word will be open to us.

The Kingdom

After Christ's incarnation, John the Baptist came out to proclaim the kingdom. From that time to the end of the New Testament, the line of the kingdom goes on without interruption. We can see the unbroken line of the kingdom throughout the remaining books of the New Testament. John the Baptist was the first one to proclaim the glad tidings of the New Testament, and the first word uttered by him was, "Repent, for the kingdom of the heavens has drawn near" (Matt. 3:2). When the Lord Jesus began His ministry, He spoke the same word (4:17). The disciples sent by the Lord were instructed by Him also to pronounce the same thing. Therefore, the second main point in the New Testament is the kingdom with its requirements.

As we have seen, a definition of the kingdom was given by the Lord in Matthew 6. At the end of His prayer, He said, "For Yours is the kingdom and the power and the glory forever" (v. 13). Power here indicates authority. In a kingdom there are two things—authority and glory. Authority deals with the enemy, and the glory expresses the Ruler, God Himself. If we read the New Testament again with the point of view of the kingdom, we will see the matters of authority and glory.

The Real Condition of Fallen Man

The third main item revealed in the four Gospels is the real condition of the fallen human race. We cannot see this picture as clearly in the other books of the New Testament. In the four Gospels there are many stories and cases that reveal to us the miserable condition of fallen mankind. These four books tell us that wherever the Lord Jesus went, He encountered sins, misery, sickness, weakness, death, demon-possession, and the evil power of darkness. These are the characteristics, the real condition, of the fallen human race.

When we read the four Gospels, our eyes are opened to see the true condition of our race.

The All-sufficiency of Christ

Fourth, these four books reveal the all-sufficiency of this God-man, Jesus. There was not one need that He could not meet nor one case or problem that He could not solve. No matter what kind of need or trouble we have, He is the unique solution.

The Wonderful Life and Living of Jesus

The four Gospels also reveal the wonderful living of the Lord Jesus. The book of Matthew shows us a life that brings in the reality of the kingdom and enables us to fulfill the requirements of this kingdom. In Mark this life brings in the real obedience to God. Luke's Gospel reveals a life which is able to make us a genuine, proper, and normal man before God and among men. In John, this life is able to express God and live out God through the human life and nature. These are the four aspects of the living of Christ in the four Gospels. This is the fifth item mentioned in the Gospels. If we see these items, the Gospels will be very clear to us.

The Impartation of the Divine Life through the Redemption of Christ

Sixth, the four Gospels tell us that this wonderful life was imparted into man based upon the redemptive work of Christ. Redemption is necessary for the impartation of the divine life.

In order to understand redemption and life-impartation, we may use the illustration of a drama. The story of the Scriptures may be compared to a drama. A wise playwright makes his drama interesting by means of a straight line through the story, along with many twists. If we look into the Scriptures in this way, we first can realize that God has an eternal purpose, which extends like a straight line from eternity past to eternity future. God's eternal purpose and heart's desire is that He would impart Himself into His creation. He wants to mingle Himself with man, to make Himself one with man, so that He becomes man's life and content, and man becomes

His expression. In this sense, man may be compared to a bottle to be filled up with God as the living water.

In order to realize this eternal purpose, God came in and created many items with man as the center. In God's creation man is the very center because man is the vessel to contain God, while all the other items of creation merely provide the environment for man, the central figure. After God created man, He put man before the tree of life, which symbolizes God Himself as life to man. God's intention was that man would eat of this tree and receive God Himself into him as his life. Thus, God's purpose would be fulfilled. At this very juncture, however, God's enemy, Satan, came in and captured, corrupted, and damaged man. This is the first, downward twist as a distraction from the straight line of God's eternal purpose.

Therefore, God Himself came to be a man. Christ came to the very place where man was, and through His redemption God brought man back to the tree of life. The redemption of Christ for the recovery of fallen man is the upward twist in the line of God's original intention. This shows us the position of God's redemption in the overall picture of His purpose.

By Christ's redemption, the fallen and distracted man was redeemed, recovered, and brought back to the tree of life. Then by Christ's resurrection this wonderful One imparted Himself into man. From this time on, man had something within him that he never had before. Before the fall, man was merely man, but now something has been added to man, that is, God Himself in Christ. Man was not only brought back to the tree of life, but the life of God was added to man. This is life-impartation.

This entire picture shows us the position of redemption. Most Christians today neglect the tree of life and pay their full attention to the "twists," the aspect of redemption. They stress the fact that man fell and became sinful. They speak of man's going to hell and of his need for salvation. It is wonderful and precious to speak of God's love for the fallen race and the shedding of Christ's blood on the cross to redeem us. However, the redemptive work is part of the twists and not on the straight line of God's intention. Today's Christianity has missed the mark, the goal of God's purpose. Very few

Christians today are clear about the straight line, that is, the eternal purpose of God, and because of this they emphasize the twists. In these last days we have the deep impression that the Lord will recover this straight line. He will make it the foremost matter, and He will make redemption the secondary matter. By all of the above, we can see the position of the life-imparting of Christ and the role of redemption.

When the Lord established His table, He said of the wine, "Drink of it, all of you, for this is My blood of the covenant, which is being poured out for many for the forgiveness of sins" (Matt. 26:27-28). However, although the Lord stressed redemption, He did not forget the straight line. Therefore, He first said of the bread, "Take, eat; this is My body" (v. 26). "My body" is on the straight line of God's eternal goal, while "My blood" for redemption is on the twists.

Man Brought into God

Man's being brought into God is the last major item unveiled in the four Gospels. The four Gospels describe a two-way traffic—the coming and going of Christ. The coming of Christ is in incarnation, and His going is in death, resurrection, and ascension. Christ's coming in incarnation brought God into man, and His going by death, resurrection, and ascension brought man into God. By His coming, God lived on earth in a man, while His going brought man into God. Therefore, man today is in the heavens in God. This is why the apostle Paul told us that our life has been hidden with Christ in God (Col. 3:3).

John 14 through 17 makes this matter more clear. Chapters fourteen through sixteen record the last words spoken by the Lord before His death, and John 17 records the Lord's closing prayer after His message. These four chapters give us a clear vision of the way in which the Lord brings us into the Father by His death, resurrection, and ascension.

HAVING THE PROPER INSIGHT
INTO THE NEW TESTAMENT

If we do not have the proper insight, we cannot be clear about what the New Testament says. Before I came to the

United States for the first time, I purchased a very good Japanese camera, and I read the instruction booklet several times. Eventually, however, I did not know what it was talking about because I did not have the insight into how the camera worked. In the same way, we may be able to recite the New Testament word by word from the first book to the last, but if we do not have the proper insight, we cannot understand it clearly and thoroughly. If we do not have the kind of insight revealed in these seven foregoing points, we can never be clear about the New Testament.

We need a clear view of Christ's incarnation, the kingdom, the condition of the fallen race, the all-sufficiency of Christ, the wonderful living of the divine life in the human life, the imparting of life through the redemption of Christ, and the wonderful fact that man has been brought into God by Christ's death, resurrection, and ascension. If we are clear concerning these few matters, God's eternal purpose and the entire holy Word will be transparent to us. This will greatly influence our daily walk and even revolutionize our entire Christian concept. Our work and our service will be greatly affected. We will be delivered from tradition and be brought into something living and real.

According to the histories and biographies of the men of God who were used very much by the Lord in the past, they had this kind of realization and insight to some degree. Of course, what they realized at their time was not as clear as what we see today, because the Lord has opened these matters more and more over the years, sometimes more and more each day. When the Lord's eternal purpose and His Word are thoroughly transparent to us, this vision will govern our walk, our work, our service, and our entire Christian concept.

CHAPTER FIVE

THE BASIC THOUGHT OF THE GOSPEL OF JOHN

Scripture Reading: John 14:1-20, 23; 15:4a; 16:19-23; 20:19-22

In this chapter we will continue our general sketch of the New Testament by looking into the Gospel of John, especially chapters fourteen through sixteen. Before proceeding, however, there is a need to make several points clear.

First of all, the Gospel of John is constructed in a certain historical sequence, especially with respect to eternity. The other three Gospels—Matthew, Mark, and Luke—are not arranged in this way. John's Gospel has the best historical arrangement, for it starts from the beginning in eternity past and it continues indefinitely into the future. Even after the last chapter, the record of this Gospel is not finished, for the history recorded in it has no end.

Second, John's record reveals to us how God comes into man and brings man into Himself. Hence, in this book there is the coming and going of the wonderful Christ. As we have seen, by His coming He brought God into man to live as a man on this earth, and by His going He brought man into God, causing man to be one with God and enabling man to live in God. This is the content of this Gospel. The Gospel of John is a record of these two main items—the coming and going of this wonderful One.

Third, the Gospel of John is divided into two main sections. The first section is composed mostly of the first twelve chapters and shows how Christ came through incarnation to bring God into man. This is His coming. The second part, chapters fourteen through twenty-one, unveils how Christ went through death and resurrection to bring man into God.

This is His going. Chapter thirteen is a turning point that divides the book into two parts. In order to understand the second section, we must know the first section. If we are going to understand His going, we must know His coming.

CHRIST COMING THROUGH INCARNATION TO BRING GOD INTO MAN

John 1 starts from the very beginning, that is, from eternity past. This wonderful One in eternity past was the Word, God Himself (v. 1). At a certain point He created the heavens and the earth, and following creation He came in incarnation to be a man in time and lived on this earth (vv. 3, 14). Then the Lord unveiled the kingdom with its requirements, He exposed the real condition of the fallen race, and He manifested His all-sufficiency. From chapter three through chapter eleven, there are nine cases in which on the one hand, man's condition is thoroughly exposed, and on the other hand, Christ's all-sufficiency is fully applied to meet the need of every man's case.

The first case is one of regeneration in life, related to Nicodemus (2:23—3:36). In the second case the Lord talked with a Samaritan woman (4:1-42). The first case deals with a good man, whereas the second case concerns an immoral woman. The third case is related to the need of the dying (vv. 43-54), and following this is the record of an impotent man who had been sick for thirty-eight years (ch. 5). Although the sick man knew what to do, he lacked the strength to do it, being weak to the uttermost.

The next case is related to a hungry crowd around the sea (ch. 6). The sea signifies a situation in which there is no peace and no satisfaction, in which people are hungry and troubled all the time. The Lord Jesus is the only one who can satisfy our hunger and calm the storm. Therefore, we must eat Him and receive Him into our boat. Following this, John 7 gives us a picture of thirsty people. To be thirsty is more serious than to be hungry. The Lord Jesus is the only one who can afford us the living word to quench our thirst.

The seventh case tells us of a guilty, dirty, and sinful woman, who was caught in adultery (7:53—8:59). Here,

Christ is the One who is able to forgive, deliver, and release people from the bondage of sin. The eighth case concerns a man who was born blind (ch. 9). Although we are born in darkness, Christ is the one who is the light of life. The last case involves Lazarus who died and was buried (ch. 11). In this situation, the Lord is the resurrection life. The final need of man in the first section of John's Gospel is resurrection. We are not only sinful and blind but dead. Therefore, we need the resurrection life. If we look into these nine cases, we can realize that they give us a full picture of man's condition and need and of how Christ is the all-sufficient One who meets the need of man's every case.

Then after the case of resurrection, we come to chapter twelve. Because Christ manifested Himself as such a wonderful One, many people came to Him and warmly welcomed Him. However, He told them that He, as the one grain of wheat, had to die in order to be multiplied as the many grains (v. 24). All the foregoing events were His coming to bring God into man to meet all of man's needs. Now at the end of His coming He declared that He needed to go by death and resurrection for the purpose of multiplication. This is the first main section of the Gospel of John.

A TURNING POINT

John 13 is a pivotal chapter in this book. This chapter is very wonderful. We should not understand it as merely a chapter on foot-washing. It is not that simple; rather, it is very deep. In this crucial chapter as the turning point of this book, the Lord did one main thing; that is, He washed the disciples' feet. He did not wash other parts but only their feet, the part that is constantly in contact with the earth. This was to cleanse them of their earthly touch. Although it is easy to become dirty by the earthly touch, the Lord has a way to cleanse us.

CHRIST GOING THROUGH DEATH AND RESURRECTION TO BRING MAN INTO GOD

After washing His disciples' feet, the Lord told them that He was going to leave them (v. 33). The disciples were

bothered and grieved when they heard that this wonderful
One was going to leave (vv. 36-37). Following this, John 14
begins the second main section of this Gospel.

Christ's coming and going are matters not of places but of
persons. Christ's intention in coming to the earth was not to
come to the earth as a place but to come into man. He was
incarnated to live not on the earth, strictly speaking, but in
man. Man, the person, is the focus. If Christ were not in man,
He would not live on this earth. Christ's coming was to be in
man.

In principle, it is the same with His going. Christ's going
was not a matter of bringing us to another, better place. His
going was to bring us into another person. We must be clear
about this basic concept. Christ's going was not to bring us to
heaven; it was to bring us into another, wonderful person, the
divine person, God the Father Himself. Just as His coming
was to bring God not merely to the earth but into man, so His
going was to bring us not to heaven but into God. If Christ
desired to bring us into heaven, He Himself would have to
remain in heaven, but at the end of the Gospel of John this
wonderful Christ is not only in the heavens but in and with
His disciples on the earth (ch. 21).

The Many Abodes in the Father's House

John 14:1 says, "Do not let your heart be troubled; believe
into God, believe also into Me." It is rather difficult for us to
understand what is meant by "believe into God, believe also
into Me." This word signifies that Christ is one with God, and
He is God. If we believe in God, we must know that the Lord
Jesus is God and that He is one with God. Here the Lord
seemed to be saying, "Since you know that I am one with God,
you should not be troubled by My going."

The Father's House Being
the Habitation of God among His People

The Lord continued in verse 2, "In My Father's house are
many abodes." What is the Father's house? Some say that this
refers to heaven. Even J. N. Darby, one of the great Bible
teachers, taught in this way. However, we must follow the

principle that the Scripture must be interpreted by its own words. In the Gospel of John the phrase *My Father's house* is used twice. The first time it appears is in chapter two verses 15 and 16 which say, "And having made a whip out of cords, He drove them all out of the temple, as well as the sheep and the oxen, and He poured out the money of the moneychangers and overturned their tables. And to those who were selling the doves He said, Take these things away from here; do not make My Father's house a house of merchandise." Since *My Father's house* in chapter two refers to the temple, could the same term refer to heaven in chapter fourteen? This is not the proper, logical way to interpret the Scriptures. The Father's house does not refer to heaven.

Many Christians expect to go to heaven, using mainly John 14 as their basis. They say that according to verse 2 a wonderful mansion is prepared for us in heaven. For two thousand years the work has been going on and still has not been finished; therefore, they say, how wonderful that mansion will be! At least one Christian hymn tells us that of all the mansions prepared in the heavens there is one for me. According to the Gospel of John itself, however, there are no such mansions. The mansions in heaven are merely of people's imagination.

The correct meaning of *My Father's house* is the very habitation of God among His people on this earth. The principle of the temple is that on this earth among God's people there is a dwelling place for God. Verse 19 in chapter two says, "Jesus answered and said to them, Destroy this temple, and in three days I will raise it up." Although the Jewish people destroyed "this temple," the Lord raised it up in three days. *This temple* refers to the Lord's physical body, which He raised in three days (v. 21). However, according to 1 Peter 1:3, all the believers were regenerated through the resurrection of Christ, and Ephesians 2:5-6 says that we were made alive together with Christ and raised up together with Him. Therefore, we also were raised up on the third day in resurrection. Christ not only raised up Himself, but He included all His believers in His resurrection. Therefore, after Christ's resurrection, God's temple is no longer Christ Himself alone. It includes all of His members, His people, as His corporate Body. This is the temple, and this is the house of God (1 Cor. 3:16-17; 1 Tim. 3:15). It is also God's habitation (Eph. 2:21-22) and "My Father's house." Strictly speaking, the Father's house is the church, which was raised up in Christ's resurrection.

The Many Abodes Being Persons, Not Places

By comparing the uses of the word *abode* throughout the same Gospel, we can arrive at its proper meaning. The King James Version renders the word *abodes* in John 14:2 as *mansions,* but this is a poor translation. In verse 23 the Lord Jesus said, "If anyone loves Me, he will keep My word, and My Father will love him, and We will come to him and make an abode with him." In Greek, the singular word *abode* in verse 23 is *mone,* the same word translated by some in the plural as *mansions* in verse 2. Moreover, the verb form of this word, *meno,* is found in 15:4, which says, "Abide in Me and I in you."

The correct usage of *abode* is found in 14:23, which says that if someone loves the Son, the Father and the Son will come to him and make an abode with him. To be sure, the abode mentioned here is a matter of persons, not a place. How then can the same word refer to persons in verse 23 and to "heavenly mansions" in verse 2? This is not a sound interpretation.

The many "mansions" are in actuality many abodes. In the Father's house, which is the temple, there are many members, and every member is an abode. This thought is very deep. In John 14 the Lord was about to die and resurrect, and by His death and resurrection He made us all a part of the temple, which is the Father's house. Before His death, we were simply the old man, having nothing to do with God's temple. However, through His death and resurrection we were made a part of, that is, members of, this temple.

Bringing the Disciples into the Father, Where Christ Is

John 14:2b-3 says, "I go to prepare a place for you. And if I go and prepare a place for you, I am coming again." The King

James Version translates "I am coming again" as "I will come again," and some interpret this to refer to the Lord's second coming. If we are not clear about the grammatical construction of verse 3, we cannot properly understand it. This verse does not say that Christ will come but that He is coming, indicating that His going was His coming.

Perhaps none of us have ever said, "If I go, I am coming"; apparently, this is a peculiar construction. However, while the Lord was going, He was coming. According to the concept of the Gospel of John, the Lord's going was His dying. The Lord was saying, "If I go to die, I am coming back." Clearly then, His coming back refers to His resurrection. In the evening of the day of resurrection Christ came back to His disciples.

Verse 3b says, "I am coming again and will receive you to Myself." This verse says that He would receive the disciples not into the heavens but to Himself. Even at the very time that the Lord was speaking to the disciples, they were still not in Him. Rather, they were outside of Him. Now the Lord was going to do something to bring them into Himself. This is the proper meaning of this verse. Jesus was going to do something to enable Him to receive them into Himself.

Verses 3-6 continue, "So that where I am you also may be. And where I am going you know the way. Thomas said to Him, Lord, we do not know where You are going; how can we know the way? Jesus said to him, I am the way and the reality and the life; no one comes to the Father except through Me." Our thought may have been that no one comes to heaven except through Jesus, but this verse says that the One to whom we come is the Father.

Verses 10-11 say, "Do you not believe that I am in the Father and the Father is in Me? The words that I say to you I do not speak from Myself, but the Father who abides in Me does His works. Believe Me that I am in the Father and the Father is in Me; but if not, believe because of the works themselves." At that time, where was the Lord? Jesus did not say, "I am in heaven." Rather, He said, "I am in the Father." Moreover, in verse 3 He had said, "Where I am you also may be." The Lord was about to do something to bring the disciples to the Father, where He was.

Then in verses 16-18 Jesus says, "And I will ask the Father, and He will give you another Comforter, that He may be with you forever, even the Spirit of reality, whom the world cannot receive, because it does not behold Him or know Him; but you know Him, because He abides with you and shall be in you. I will not leave you as orphans; I am coming to you." "I am coming to you" is different from "I will come to you," as the King James Version says. The former indicates that while the Lord was speaking this word, He was already on the way; He was already coming.

The Lord Coming on "That Day," the Day of Resurrection

In verses 19 to 20 the Lord goes on to say, "Yet a little while and the world beholds Me no longer, but you behold Me; because I live, you also shall live. In that day you will know that I am in My Father, and you in Me, and I in you." *That day* is the day of resurrection, not the day of His second coming in the future.

To understand the meaning of *that day,* it is sufficient to look at other passages in this same Gospel. John 16:16-17 says, "A little while and you no longer behold Me, and again a little while and you will see Me. Some of His disciples then said to one another, What is this that He says to us, A little while and you do not behold Me, and again a little while and you will see Me; and, Because I am going to the Father?" In verses 20-23 Jesus replied, "Truly, truly, I say to you that you will weep and lament, but the world will rejoice; you will be sorrowful, but your sorrow will be turned into joy. A woman, when she gives birth, has sorrow because her hour has come; but when she brings forth the little child, she no longer remembers the affliction because of the joy that a man has been born into the world. Therefore you also now have sorrow; but I will see you again and your heart will rejoice, and no one takes your joy away from you. And in that day you will ask Me nothing." The disciples wept and lamented at the time the Lord was crucified, but their sorrow was turned into joy when the child was delivered on "that day," the day of resurrection. The disciples were then like a woman travailing in birth, and

Christ was the child to be brought forth in His resurrection (Acts 13:33; Heb. 1:5; Rom. 1:4).

Chapter twenty also speaks of *that day*. Verses 19 and 20 say, "When therefore it was evening on that day, the first day of the week, and while the doors were shut where the disciples were for fear of the Jews, Jesus came and stood in the midst and said to them, Peace be to you. And when He had said this, He showed them His hands and His side. The disciples therefore rejoiced at seeing the Lord." This portion of the Scriptures is the fulfillment of the word spoken by the Lord in chapters fourteen through sixteen. The Lord came back on "that day," the day of resurrection.

Christ in Resurrection Breathing into and Remaining in the Disciples

Sending the Disciples by Being in Them

Verse 21 says, "Then Jesus said to them again, Peace be to you; as the Father has sent Me, I also send you." In what way did the Father send the Son? The Father sent the Son by being in the Son. Now the Son was sending His disciples in the same way, that is, by being in them. Therefore, verse 22 continues, "And when He had said this, He breathed into them and said to them, Receive the Holy Spirit." By breathing into them, He Himself as the Holy Spirit came into them. The Holy Spirit is the very breath that the Lord breathed. The Lord seemed to be saying, "I send you by breathing into you. This is the way the Father sent Me; He sent Me with Himself. When I was sent by the Father, I had the Father within Me, and He was one with Me. Now I send you in the same way; that is, I am entering into you to be one with you." After He said this, He breathed the Holy Spirit into them. That breath was simply Christ Himself.

Remaining with the Disciples in a Mysterious, Wonderful Way

After saying this, the record in John 20 does not say that the Lord Jesus left the disciples. This portion of the word tells us three times that He came (vv. 19, 24, 26), but not once do chapters twenty or twenty-one say that Jesus left the disciples. Rather, He remained in them as the living breath. Therefore, wherever they were, He was there also. If they were in the room, He was in the room also. If they were at the seashore, He was at the seashore too (ch. 21). It is not that the Lord left them but that He was either invisible or manifested. Even without appearing to manifest Himself, He was still there.

After His resurrection, Christ came to His disciples in order to come into them. This transpired while the doors and windows were closed because at that time the disciples were in fear of the Jews (20:19). Although the doors and windows of the room were shut, Jesus came in. It seems that He must have come as the Spirit, but He showed them His hands and His side (v. 20). This indicates that He still had a physical body. How could He with a physical body enter the room with the doors closed? This is something wonderful which is beyond our understanding. We cannot understand in a full way how He came, but the fact is that after He resurrected, He came back to the disciples. Moreover, there is no word here that tells us that He left again. Rather, after He came, He remained there in a wonderful way. His coming, His presence, is very mysterious, wonderful, and beyond our understanding. We should not try to analyze it and understand it by our natural mentality; we should simply receive the word of John 20.

Coming as "Another Comforter"

In John 14:16 the Lord said that the Father would give the disciples another Comforter. Some Christian teachers say that this word was fulfilled on the day of Pentecost (Acts 2:1-4). This is a wrong interpretation. Acts 2 refers to the baptism in the Spirit. On the day of resurrection the Lord breathed the Spirit into the disciples for their life, while on the day of Pentecost the Spirit as the rushing, violent wind blew upon the disciples for power. These are two different aspects of the one Spirit. When the apostle John wrote his Gospel, he did not do so with Acts 2 in view. On the contrary, the Gospel of John is a complete book showing us that the Triune God was incarnated to be a man, bringing Himself into man, mingling Himself with man, and living on this earth as a man. He went into death, and in resurrection He imparted Himself into man. Then through His resurrection and ascension, He brought man into God. From this point on, God is in man and man is in God. He and man are one.

John 14:17 tells us that the Comforter was first with the disciples and then in them. By reading the following verses again and again, we can understand that the Spirit as "another Comforter" is none other than Christ Himself in another form. We must pay close attention to these verses. In verses 17-18 the Lord spoke of the Spirit of reality, saying, "He abides with you and shall be in you. I will not leave you as orphans; I am coming to you." From verse 17 to verse 18, the pronoun quickly changes from "He" to "I." The very *He* who is the Spirit of reality in verse 17, becomes the very *I* who is the Lord Himself in verse 18. It is a matter of form; at that time the Lord was in the form of the flesh, but after His death and resurrection He was transfigured into the Spirit. We may illustrate this by water and vapor. Although water becomes vapor, the essence of the water is still the same; it is different only in form.

Before the Lord's death and resurrection He was a man in the flesh. In the form of flesh He could not enter into His disciples, so He had to be transformed, transfigured, into another form. After His death and resurrection, He could enter into His disciples in a mysterious way, a way which we cannot understand in full. He came into the room with the doors closed, yet with a physical body; this is wonderful and mysterious. Now He was able to breathe Himself into His disciples. From that time forth the disciples had the Holy Spirit within them.

If the disciples did not have this wonderful Spirit within them, how could the one hundred twenty pray for ten days together in one accord (Acts 1:14)? Moreover, at that time in Jerusalem there was a strong threatening by the Jews. Whoever followed Jesus was persecuted, but these Galilean fishermen were not afraid. They gave up their homes and families in order to remain in Jerusalem. Then they stayed together and prayed for ten days in one accord, and Peter could even understand the prophecies of the Psalms (v. 20). Who gave them this boldness and ability? It was the indwelling Spirit.

At the time of John 20, however, they had the indwelling Spirit, but they lacked the outpouring of the Spirit. They enjoyed the inward aspect but lacked the outward aspect. They drank of the Spirit within, yet they had no outward clothing, no uniform without. They needed the Spirit of power as the uniform in order to exercise authority. For this, they had to wait until the day of Pentecost. This is the second aspect of the Spirit; it is not the aspect that the Gospel of John reveals.

Christ's Coming and Going
to Produce the Mutual Dwelling of God and Man

The Gospel of John reveals that the Father is in the Son, coming to be among humanity, and the Son became the Spirit to enter into humanity. His entering into man was accomplished by means of His going in death and His coming in resurrection. Christ's going was not to leave the disciples but a further step to come into them. By the first step of incarnation He came to be among them. After that, He needed to take another step to enter into them. Incarnation was the first step of His coming, and death and resurrection was the second step.

Apparently Christ's death was His going, but actually it was His coming. His going to die did not mean that He left the disciples. It only means that He took another step to get into them. Therefore, the Lord could say, "If I go...I am coming" (14:3). He seemed to be saying, "Do not be sorrowful. Do not think that I am going to leave you. I have come to you, but at this time I am only among you. This is only the first step; I cannot yet enter into you. I must do something further so that I can be in you. I must take a further step to die and resurrect. After death and resurrection, I will then be able to enter into you. Therefore, My going is My coming." For this reason, the Gospel of John does not say that after Christ died and resurrected, He left the disciples. Instead, it tells us that after

He died and resurrected, He came to them and entered into them.

In verse 20 the Lord said, "In that day you will know that I am in My Father, and you in Me, and I in you," and in verse 3 He said, "Where I am you also may be." On "that day" the disciples would be where the Lord is. Where is the Lord? He is in the Father. Therefore, in that day they would be in the Father also. While the Lord was speaking this, they were not yet in the Father because Christ had not yet died and resurrected. The Lord was still in the form of the flesh. He needed to die and resurrect, and after His death and resurrection, He was transfigured into the Spirit. Then, at that time He was able to enter into the disciples. Since the Lord was in the Father and they were in Him, spontaneously they were also in the Father. It is in this way that the Lord brought them into the Father. Now where the Lord is, we are there also.

In this way God becomes our abode, and we become God's abode, so in the following chapter there is the mutual abiding. John 15:4 says, "Abide in Me and I in you." By His coming in incarnation, Christ brought God into man, and by His going through death and resurrection He brought man into God. Now God and man, man and God, become a mutual abode. We abide in God, and God abides in us. The way has been paved, and the fact has been accomplished. Now we simply enjoy this mutual abiding. Now, in the Father's house, that is, in the temple of God, the church, each one of us not only has a place, but each one of us is a "place." We not only have an abode; each one is an abode.

In Revelation 21 and 22 it is difficult to see who the dwellers are in the New Jerusalem. The twelve apostles are not, strictly speaking, the dwellers there; they are the foundations. We may compare them to bricks in a building. We do not say that bricks dwell in the building; they are only part of the building. But in another sense, the building becomes the dwelling place of the bricks. Similarly, when we are built into the church, the building of God becomes our dwelling place. All of the saved and redeemed ones are parts of the New Jerusalem. Who then is the dweller? It is the Triune God.

The Real Meaning of John 14 and 20

John 14 and 20 should now be very clear. At that time the Lord Jesus was able only to be among the disciples; He was not able to enter into them. Therefore, the Lord needed to die and resurrect, and in so doing, He was transfigured from the flesh into the Spirit, who is a wonderful person (1 Cor. 15:45b). After His resurrection, the Lord still had a physical body, yet it was wonderful and mysterious. On the day of resurrection, He came to the disciples in this extraordinary way, not only to be with the disciples but also to enter into them as breath. He breathed into them and said, "Receive the Holy Spirit" (John 20:22). Just as the Father sent the Son, the Lord was also in the disciples and one with them to send them.

After His death and resurrection, the Lord Himself is not only in the Father but also in the disciples. Since the disciples are in the Lord, and the Lord is in the disciples, they are automatically in the Father. Therefore, where the Lord is, there the disciples are also. In this way the Lord brought them into God. Now everything has been accomplished. God is in man, and man is in God, so God and man become a mutual abode. God becomes our abode, and we become God's abode mutually. For this reason, John 15 continues with the Lord's word to abide in Him and He in us. This is the proper meaning of this portion of John.

Being in the Father but Going to the Father

On the one hand, John 14:10 tells us that the Lord is in the Father, while on the other hand, the Lord needed to go to the Father (vv. 12, 28). When the Lord Jesus was on this earth, according to His divinity, His inward essence, He was already in the Father. However, He also had another part, another nature, which is His humanity, which had not yet been transfigured to be in the Father. Therefore, He had to pass through death and resurrection. By passing through death and resurrection, His humanity was transfigured and brought into His divinity.

KNOWING THE BASIC THOUGHT OF THIS GOSPEL
AND OF THE ENTIRE NEW TESTAMENT

In order to understand the Gospel of John we must be very careful. We should not understand this portion of the Word by our human concept. This is a mistake made by so many Christian teachers. We have pointed out, for example, that many Christians teach that John 14 speaks about going to heaven, but this is inconsistent with the context of the entire Gospel of John. The context of this entire book tells us that first God was incarnated to be a m an, and then He brought man into Himself by the death, resurrection, and ascension of Christ. Our intention in stressing this matter is not merely to adjust and correct the wrong teachings in Christianity. It is to see something subjective in life. We must realize that it is not the Lord's intention to prepare a place for us in the heavens and then one day to bring us there. This is not the thought of God. The thought of God today is to work Himself into us. We must realize how much we need to be wrought into God and have Christ wrought into us. May we all be clear that this is the basic thought of this Gospel and the basic thought of the entire New Testament.

CHAPTER SIX

CHRIST, THE SPIRIT, AND THE BODY
IN THE BOOK OF ACTS

Scripture Reading: Acts 9:1-17; 22:6-16; 1 Cor. 12:13; Luke 24:49; John 7:37-39

In the previous chapters we saw seven main points relating to the content of the four Gospels. These are incarnation, the kingdom, the condition of man, Christ meeting every man's needs, the divine living in humanity, the imparting of Christ as life, and man being brought into God. Although these matters may seem brief and simple, they are very profound. Therefore, we need to spend more time to pray over these points and to ask the Lord to reveal something further in order that we may thoroughly understand the spiritual content of these four books.

Now we may come to the book of Acts. As we have mentioned previously, the Acts should not be separated from the four Gospels. The Acts should be included with the Gospels because these five books together give us a full picture of a universal man. The four Gospels give us a picture of the Head, and the book of Acts shows us the Body.

THE DUPLICATION AND REPRODUCTION OF CHRIST

The books of the Scriptures were not originally given their titles by their writers. The titles were given by others many years later when they arranged the books of the Scriptures. In some versions of the Bible, the book of Acts is simply called *The Acts,* but in the King James Version it is called *The Acts of the Apostles.* Strictly speaking, however, this book records not merely the acts of the apostles but the acts of Christ by the Spirit in the church. The acts of the apostles and of all the believers, that is, of the church, are the acts of Christ in the church by the Holy Spirit.

In the four Gospels there is one man, Jesus of Nazareth, living in a divine way by the divine life. In the Acts, however, there are thousands of persons living in a divine way by the same divine life. In the four Gospels there is a single Jew who lived divinely, but in the Acts there are thousands of Jews and Gentiles living exactly in the same way as He did. Moreover, these thousands of people lived, acted, walked, and worked not by themselves but by that one wonderful person. After the Lord Jesus died, resurrected, and ascended, He continued to live, act, walk, and work on this earth in thousands of people because He imparted Himself into them through His death and resurrection. By His death, resurrection, and ascension, He made a mass reproduction of Himself. Originally He was one Jesus, one Christ, but now He was reproduced in thousands of Christians. Originally He was one grain, but now He became many grains, a mass duplication, a mass reproduction (John 12:24). Every one of us is also a part of this mass reproduction.

We may illustrate this duplication by the printing of a newspaper. There are three main steps in the printing process. The first step is the thought of what we want to print. The thought is the very source; without a thought there is nothing to put into black and white. However, the thought is invisible, unexpressed, unknown, hidden, mysterious, and secret. The thought may be compared to the Father in the Triune God (John 1:18a; 2 Cor. 13:14).

Following this, the thought becomes the word, which is written and composed as the *logos* in a particular language, that is, into a literate, expressed writing. This is the second step, which includes many items. After the word is written and composed into expressed writings, it is typeset and put on a printing plate. Everything that is in the thought is now visible with a definite form. This may be compared to the Son in the Triune God as the expression of God (John 1:1, 14, 18b).

The third step is the duplication in which the plate is placed on the press with the ink. Millions of copies can then be reproduced from the one plate. What is printed on the copies is identical to what is on the plate. In the evening there is only the thought, but by the next morning millions of people can read what is in the newspaper as the reproduction of the thought. The printing with the ink may be compared to the Holy Spirit, and we are the many sheets of paper (2 Cor. 3:3, 18).

This process points to the person and work of Christ. First, He is the Word of God to express God. By His incarnation, His human living on this earth, His sufferings, and His death and resurrection, all that He is was "typeset" and put on the "printing plate." In printing, the plate is a real treasure. If we intend to print a book, we must finish the plate first. After it is finished, we can keep it and use it to duplicate many copies whenever we need them. In this way, it is easy to reproduce millions of copies. The thought to be printed can be compared to the Father, the plate signifies the Son, the duplicating illustrates the Holy Spirit, and we, the believers, are the copies.

When Christ died, resurrected, and ascended, the plate was made. Following this, many copies were reproduced by the Holy Spirit. The Holy Spirit printed the image on the plate onto Peter and John and onto us today. We are like blank pieces of paper onto which the Holy Spirit prints whatever is on the plate. From the day of resurrection until today millions of copies have been printed by the Holy Spirit with Himself.

Whatever Christ is, is the printing plate as the expression of the thought, that is, of the Father. Therefore, on the plate, which is Christ, we can read the thought of the Father. On Christ, in Christ, and with Christ, we can see the expression of the Father. Moreover, others can read the same thing in us, the many pieces of paper, that they read in Christ because whatever is on the plate has been reproduced in us. We are the reproduction of Christ.

In brief, in the four Gospels, there is the printing plate, and in the Acts we find the duplication, the reproduction. Therefore, the Acts are the Acts of Christ, not Christ acting in Himself alone but acting in His reproduction and duplication, which is the church, the Body of the universal man. This universal man is the fullness of Christ (Eph. 1:23); therefore, it is a part of Christ, even Christ Himself.

CHRIST LIVING AND MOVING IN HIS BODY

We may now examine two portions from Acts. Acts 9 has ministered much life to me. Verses 1 and 2 say, "But Saul, still breathing threatening and murder against the disciples of the Lord, went to the high priest and asked for letters from him to Damascus for the synagogues, so that if he found any who were of the Way, both men and women, he might bring them bound to Jerusalem." It is noteworthy how the Holy Spirit uses the term *the Way* in verse 2. The disciples were not in a doctrine, a teaching, or a religion but in the Way. Saul bound not those in a certain mentality but those in a certain living and walk.

Verses 3 and 4 say, "And as he went, he drew near to Damascus, and suddenly a light from heaven flashed around him. And he fell on the ground and heard a voice saying to him, Saul, Saul, why are you persecuting Me?" We must emphasize the word *Me* in verse 4. Someone from heaven came to ask Saul, "Why are you persecuting Me?" Verse 5 continues, "And he said, Who are You, Lord? And He said, I am Jesus, whom you persecute."

This word from the Lord surprised the young Saul very much. Saul could have argued, "I never persecuted anyone in the heavens, but now You are speaking from the heavens that I persecuted You. Who are You? I persecuted Stephen and many others, but I never persecuted a man by the name of Jesus." At this time, however, Saul did not argue. Rather, he received the truth concerning the Body. From the first time he met the Lord, he received the vision of the Body. He saw the vision that all those who believe in Jesus are a part of Jesus. Therefore, to persecute them is to persecute Jesus because they are one with Jesus and He is living in them. In this way, Saul of Tarsus received the revelation that the Body of Christ, including all His members, is Christ Himself (1 Cor. 12:12).

To persecute the disciples of Christ is to persecute Christ Himself, because all the disciples of Christ are the members of the Body of Christ, and the Body of Christ is Christ Himself. For someone to hit a part of my body is to hit my body, and to hit my body is to hit me. While Saul was persecuting so many believers, he never realized that he was persecuting Jesus. But when the Lord came to him, He pointed out that Saul was persecuting the Lord Himself because it was He who was moving, living, and acting in all those believers.

When Paul recounted this incident in Acts 26, he added that the Lord said, "It is hard for you to kick against the goads" (v. 14). A goad is a sharp-pointed stick used to subdue and prod an ox yoked to the plow. The Lord's word here signifies that even before Saul was met by the Lord, he was under His yoke. For this reason, Paul later said that he was set apart unto the Lord from his mother's womb (Gal. 1:15).

In Acts 9:6 the Lord said, "But rise up and enter into the city, and it will be told to you what you must do." The Lord did not tell Saul directly what he should do. Rather, the Lord told him indirectly through a member of the Body. From the first day the Lord met him, Saul was made to know the Body. Saul was put into the Body and made to realize that whatever he did to the Body he did also to the Head, and if he was to do something from the Head, he must know it through the Body. It seems as if the Lord was saying, "Saul, I will not tell you what to do directly. You must go to the city where My Body is. There, a member of the Body will come to you and tell you what to do."

Verses 7 and 8 say, "And the men who journeyed with him stood speechless, hearing the voice but seeing no one. And Saul rose from the ground; and though his eyes were open, he could see nothing. And they led him by the hand and brought him into Damascus." Formerly, Saul led other people. Now he was led by others. Verses 10-17 continue, "And there was a certain disciple in Damascus named Ananias; and the Lord said to him in a vision, Ananias. And he said, Behold, I am here, Lord. And the Lord said to him, Rise up and go to the lane called Straight, and seek in the house of Judas a man from Tarsus named Saul; for behold, he is praying; and he has seen in a vision a man named Ananias coming in and laying his hands on him so that he may receive his sight. But

Ananias answered, Lord, I have heard from many concerning this man, how many evil things he has done to Your saints in Jerusalem; and here he has authority from the chief priests to bind all who call upon Your name. But the Lord said to him, Go, for this man is a chosen vessel to Me, to bear My name before both the Gentiles and kings and the sons of Israel; for I will show him how many things he must suffer on behalf of My name. And Ananias went away and entered into the house; and laying his hands on him, he said, Saul, brother, the Lord has sent me—Jesus, who appeared to you on the road on which you were coming—so that you may receive your sight and be filled with the Holy Spirit." For Ananias to lay hands on Saul was to receive Saul into the Body. Moreover, Ananias called Saul "brother."

Acts 22 contains a similar account of Saul's calling and provides more details. In verse 8 the Lord says to Saul, "I am Jesus the Nazarene, whom you persecute." Here the Lord told Saul in a definite and specific way that He was Jesus of Nazareth. Verses 11-16 continue, "And as I could not see because of the glory of that light, I was led by the hand by those who were with me and came into Damascus. And a certain Ananias, a devout man according to the law, well attested to by all the Jews dwelling there, came to me, and standing by, said to me, Brother Saul, receive your sight! And in that very hour I looked up at him. And he said, The God of our fathers has previously appointed you to know His will and to see the righteous One and to hear the voice from His mouth; for you will be a witness to Him unto all men of the things which you have seen and heard. And now, why do you delay? Rise up and be baptized and wash away your sins, calling on His name."

By this account we again can see that from the first day that Saul met the Lord Jesus, he was enlightened to know the Body, that the Body is one with the Head, and that whatever the Lord does must be through His Body. The Lord did not call him in detail in a personal and direct way. Rather, the Lord told him to go to one of the members of His Body. It was through that member of the Body that the Lord's calling was made known to Saul in detail. Saul was called in such a way that he was made to know the church as the Body.

In principle, many of us have had a similar experience. It is difficult to know the meaning of the Lord's calling by ourselves alone. Many times we need the members of the Body to interpret the significance of the Lord's calling. This shows us that the Head Himself lives, works, and moves in the members of the Body. In this way, the work or acts of the believers, the church, are actually the acts of Christ Himself. The members of Christ live and act not by themselves but by another One, by Christ as the Spirit. They take Christ as the Spirit to be their life, strength, power, and everything, and they live by Him.

BEING FILLED INWARDLY AND CLOTHED OUTWARDLY WITH THE HOLY SPIRIT

Many Christians today have a wrong understanding concerning the baptism in the Holy Spirit (Acts 1:5). The real meaning of the baptism in the Holy Spirit is that we as human beings are immersed in God. When we are baptized by immersion, we are put under the water and buried in it to be terminated. In the same way, to be baptized in the Holy Spirit is to be immersed in the Spirit, so that whatever we are, whatever we do, and the way we live and work are not out of ourselves but by the Lord Christ as the Spirit.

There are two aspects of the Holy Spirit. On the one hand, the Holy Spirit enters into us as the indwelling Spirit; this is the inward aspect. On the other hand, we are baptized into the Spirit; this is the outward aspect. In other words, we are filled with the Spirit inwardly and immersed in the Spirit outwardly. First Corinthians 12:13 speaks of these two aspects, saying, "For also in one Spirit we were all baptized into one Body, whether Jews or Greeks, whether slaves or free, and were all given to drink one Spirit." To drink water is to take the water into us, and to be baptized is to get into the water. To get into the Spirit and to take the Spirit into us is to be completely mingled with the Triune God. The Triune God fills and occupies us within, and He covers us without. Within and without, everywhere and in everything, there is the Triune God.

In Luke 24:49 the Lord likens the Holy Spirit as power to

clothing, saying, "And behold, I send forth the promise of My Father upon you; but as for you, stay in the city until you put on power from on high." To put on the Spirit is to be clothed with the Spirit. On the other hand, in John 7:37-39 the Holy Spirit within us as life is likened to water for drinking. We must be filled with the Holy Spirit as the water of life. If we are thirsty, we need to come to the Lord Jesus to drink of Him as the Spirit. Water is something we take in, while clothing is something we put on. We have to be filled with the Triune God within, and we must put on the Triune God without. The Triune God within is our drink, and the Triune God without is our uniform.

With the uniform comes the authority. If a policeman stands on the street without a uniform, who will respect his authority? His authority rests in his uniform. If anyone puts on a police uniform and stands on the street, he can command the same respect; everyone will obey his orders. Even for doctors and nurses to carry out their responsibilities, they must wear their respective uniforms. The uniform carries with it the power, the position, and the authority. We need the baptism in the Holy Spirit because the Spirit is our uniform. We may drink something and be filled within, but if we have no uniform, no one will respect us or listen to us. People do not recognize our infilling; they only recognize our uniform. However, if we have only the uniform without the inward life supply, we are weak and have no strength to stand.

Both the inner filling and the outer clothing are God Himself. All those disciples mentioned in the book of Acts were filled with God within and clothed with God without. Everything within them and upon them was God Himself, and they were lost and buried in God. Later on in the New Testament, the apostle Paul tells us, "I am crucified with Christ; and it is no longer I who live, but it is Christ who lives in me" (Gal. 2:20). The secret and principle of the disciples' living is found in this verse. They did not live, work, or do things in themselves. Rather, they lived and did everything by another life, by Christ Himself. They were filled with Christ within, and they were clothed with Christ without; that is, they were clothed with the Spirit.

The real meaning of the baptism in the Holy Spirit is that we are immersed in God and put God on as our clothing. As Christians and members of Christ, we must be filled with Him inwardly and clothed with Him outwardly. This is what we need, and this is exactly what He is doing with us. We must be clear about this, claim it by faith, and receive it. Then we have it; we are filled within and clothed without, and in this way we are persons who are fully mingled with Him. We can live and walk by Him as life, as power, and as everything.

LIVING AND MOVING BY THE PRESENT GUIDANCE OF THE HOLY SPIRIT

The book of Acts shows us that none of the disciples did anything according to rules, regulations, or orders. They did not live or act by organization or directions from man. Neither did they live or act according to knowledge or doctrine. Even the more, they did not live according to tradition or anything old. In this book of twenty-eight chapters, there is no record that the believers acted, lived, worked, walked, or did things according to regulations, rules, organization, man's orders, doctrines, knowledge, tradition, or anything old. Rather, they lived, acted, worked, and did things according to the present guidance of the Holy Spirit. Every day they lived and moved according to the living guidance of the Holy Spirit; that is, they lived by this living One.

The disciples did not have such a thing as Christianity. They even may have not known the term *sanctification,* although they had the fact of sanctification. Today, however, we may have regulations, rules, organization, man's orders, doctrine, knowledge, traditions, and old matters, but we may not have the present, living, and fresh guidance of the Holy Spirit. We cannot have the living guidance of the Holy Spirit merely by learning doctrines. Let us forget about what we know and abandon those old things. We must have the present, living, fresh, new, up-to-date guidance from the living Lord.

Many people are still too much under the influence of the old, traditional teachings of Christianity, and they hold on to their rules, regulations, doctrines, and knowledge. Sometimes people do not agree with our messages, but I do not argue with them; arguing never works. I simply say, "If you would humble yourself before the Lord, you will see what we are speaking." It is not a matter of agreeing or not agreeing; it is a matter of seeing. Do not exercise your mind merely to agree, and do not consider everything according to rules, regulations, organization, and old doctrine and knowledge. Rather, you must see something in a deeper way.

Recently, a brother showed our hymnal to a certain missionary. When that missionary looked into the table of contents, he asked, "Do you have a category for songs about heaven?" This exemplifies how much we have been influenced by the traditional teachings, such as the traditional teaching of going to heaven. We do not know how much we have been deceived by such traditional teachings. We certainly believe that there is a heaven and that the Lord Jesus today is in the heavens, but there is no verse telling us that after we die we will go to heaven, as is taught in the traditional way. Many people pay their attention to the deceitful, traditional teachings, but they neglect the most central matters of the revelation of the Scriptures.

DENYING OURSELVES AND LIVING BY CHRIST

The book of Acts presents a picture showing us that all the members of Christ are completely one with Him. Inwardly we must be filled with Him, outwardly we must be clothed with Him, and every day we must live, walk, work, and do things not by ourselves but one hundred percent by Him. We do not live by ourselves but by Him. At all times we must reject ourselves, deny ourselves, and repudiate ourselves, and we must depend on Him for our living, doing, walking, working, and everything. We should not care for the traditions, and we should not be affected by what people say about us, whether they criticize or appreciate us. We should not fear man's "face of clay." Rather, we must take care of one thing only: We must take Christ as our life and depend on Him.

As living members of Christ, we are filled with Him within and clothed with Him without. We do not live by ourselves or for ourselves; we live by Him and for Him, and in everything we depend on Him. If we live in this way, we will be in the "twenty-ninth chapter" of Acts. We will be in the flow of the Spirit. We should forget lesser matters, such as speaking in tongues and healings and simply be filled with Christ and clothed with Christ. We must reckon ourselves as dead and depend on Him for everything. If we need healing or a certain gift, we will receive it at the right time. However, the main point is not the gift but to take Christ as everything to us and to depend on Him. We must have a clear vision that we are Christ's members who are filled with Him within and clothed with Him without. We are baptized in Him, and now we are learning to take Him as our life and depend on Him for everything. This is the proper way for us to take.

CHAPTER SEVEN

THE CRUCIAL TRANSITION
FROM THE GOSPELS TO THE ACTS

Scripture Reading: John 20:22; 1 Pet. 1:3; Acts 1:5; 2:1-4;
11:15-16; 2:36; Psa. 2:6; 1 Cor. 12:13

At the end of the four Gospels and the beginning of Acts,
there is a crucial transition. We also must pass through the
same kind of transition, not merely in the knowledge of these
matters but even more in our experience.

As we have seen, the four Gospels show us a picture of the
Lord Jesus living, walking, working, and acting on the earth
by the divine life and in the divine Spirit. In the Acts, there
are thousands of persons as His Body, the church, who live,
walk, work, and act in the same life and by the same Spirit.
The persons have changed, but the life and the Spirit are still
the same. The change is not one of life; it is one of persons.
This is the crucial transition from the Gospels to the Acts.

THE IMPARTATION OF LIFE
THROUGH THE RESURRECTION OF CHRIST

This change in persons was accomplished by the Lord's
resurrection and ascension. Resurrection is a matter of life,
whereas ascension is a matter of authority and power.
Because many Christians today are not clear about the Lord's
resurrection and His ascension, we need to speak something
further concerning these two points.

As we saw in previous chapters, by His death and resurrection, the Lord imparted Himself into us as our life. When
Christ was resurrected from the dead, we were raised up
together with Him, that is, resurrected with Him (Eph. 2:6).
Moreover, 1 Peter 1:3 says, "Blessed be the God and Father of

our Lord Jesus Christ, who according to His great mercy has regenerated us unto a living hope through the resurrection of Jesus Christ from the dead." God has regenerated us through the resurrection of Christ from the dead. Before His resurrection, Christ and we were separate, but by His resurrection Christ came into us to be our life and our very nature.

John 12:24 says, "Truly, truly, I say to you, Unless the grain of wheat falls into the ground and dies, it abides alone; but if it dies, it bears much fruit." The Lord Jesus as the one grain of wheat became many grains through His death and resurrection. For a grain of wheat to fall into the earth signifies death, and for it to grow up out of the earth signifies resurrection. Moreover, the grain of wheat grows up not merely by itself but with many other grains. Many grains are raised up and brought into life by the growth of the one grain, which signifies resurrection.

We were raised up with Christ by His resurrection and in His resurrection. Some may ask how we could have been raised with Christ before we were even born. We should not argue with the Bible. It also tells us that we died with Christ on the cross long before our birth (Rom. 6:6; Gal. 2:20a). With God there is no consideration of time; He considers everything from eternity.

As we have seen, 1 Peter 1:3 says that we have been regenerated by the resurrection of Christ. Second Peter 1:4 goes on to say, "Through which He has granted to us precious and exceedingly great promises that through these you might become partakers of the divine nature." By His resurrection, Christ imparted Himself into us not only as our life but with His divine nature. In this way we partake of the divine nature.

THE INAUGURATION WITH AUTHORITY
BY THE ASCENSION OF CHRIST

The Need for Authority, Equipping,
and Qualification

The resurrection life imparted into us is the inward aspect of life. There is also the need of something outward for authority, equipping, and qualification. All things in nature are types and signs of the spiritual things. Our physical life, for example, is a type. Although we may have a strong physical life, it is only for us to live. Our physical life is not the qualification, equipping, or authority to exercise an office. In order to carry out an office, we must be qualified, equipped, and authorized. Even though a person is living and healthy, he cannot go into the street and act as a policeman without the proper authorization. He must do something further to be qualified before he can act as a policeman with authority.

The resurrection of Christ enables us to be regenerated. It imparts Christ Himself into us as our life and nature, but His resurrection is not sufficient to equip us, qualify us, and authorize us. Therefore, we also need His ascension. Whereas resurrection is a matter of life, Christ's ascension is a matter of position, and position is a matter of authority. If we do not have the position, we can never have the authority. We can compare our position to the presidency. In the United States the president must be inaugurated. When he is inaugurated into office, he is put into a position that authorizes, equips, and qualifies him to act and exercise the power of the presidency.

By raising up Christ from the dead, God testified that Christ is life. Death can neither subdue nor hold this life (Acts 2:24). This life is an indestructible life which can never be destroyed or damaged by anything (Heb. 7:16). This was proved and testified by Christ's resurrection. By Christ's ascension, however, God testified that Christ is the Lord, the Head, and the King (Acts 2:36; Eph. 1:22; Rev. 19:16). In reference to this, Psalm 2:6 says, "But I have installed My King / Upon Zion, My holy mountain." Christ is the Head, the Lord, and the King of kings. As the anointed One, all power and authority have been committed and entrusted to Him. He is the very center of God's authority, power, administration, and government, and now He is on the throne. This was accomplished in Christ's ascension. Hence, resurrection is a matter of life, while ascension is a matter of headship, lordship, kingship, authority, government, enthronement, and power.

In the evening of the day of resurrection, the Lord came to

the disciples in a very mysterious way; that is, He came to them as life. He came not openly but privately to the room where the disciples were meeting in a hidden way. None of the Lord's followers knew what was about to happen, but in a very secret and mysterious way He came to breathe Himself into them, saying, "Receive the Holy Spirit" (John 20:22). From that moment on, the disciples had this wonderful One within them as their life and nature. However, although these disciples were enlivened, regenerated, and raised up with Christ, they were still not qualified, equipped, and authorized because Christ Himself had not yet been enthroned. Not until He ascended into heaven was He enthroned. Ephesians 1:20-22 tells us that God raised Christ up and seated Him in the highest place as the Head over all things. He was enthroned and entrusted with all authority. Resurrection, therefore, is a matter of life, while ascension is a matter of authority.

The Inauguration of the Body
by the Anointing upon the Body

Today Christ is the Head and the center of all authority. After His ascension, He descended as the Spirit of power to inaugurate His disciples on the day of Pentecost (Acts 2:1-4). According to the Old Testament, whenever apprentices assumed the priesthood, they needed to be anointed. This anointing was equivalent to their inauguration. In the same way, Christ inaugurated the disciples on the day of Pentecost. That day was their inauguration day. At that time they were authorized, equipped, qualified, and placed into the position of power, and on that very day they began to assume their function.

This is the real meaning of the baptism in the Holy Spirit. The baptism in the Holy Spirit is the inauguration, the anointing, of the church. Moreover, the baptism in the Holy Spirit is not for individual believers but for the Body (1 Cor. 12:13). The Head has inaugurated the Body, not the individual members separately. In other words, He has appointed and authorized the Body to function.

Two Procedures for Our Mingling
with the Triune God

First, the Triune God—God in Christ as the Spirit—came into us as our life and nature. Second, this very Triune God who accomplished everything and put everything into Christ's hand, giving Him all authority, came down upon His Body, including all the believers, as their authority and equipping. Inwardly we have the Triune God Himself as our life, and outwardly we have the Triune God Himself as our authority. Thus, from within to without we are thoroughly mingled with the Triune God. He is our life and also our authority. We have Him not only within as our life to live Him but without as our power and authority to act, to work, and to do things.

Our mingling with the Triune God has not been fully realized by many Christians today. Although many know something about being regenerated and having eternal life, they do not see clearly that this eternal life is the very Triune God Himself within us as our life and nature. Likewise, although many realize that on the day of Pentecost the Spirit came down and baptized the disciples with power from on high, they may not realize that this power from on high is nothing other than the Triune God Himself.

By the time of Christ's ascension Christ had accomplished many things. God had mingled Himself with man in the incarnation and brought Himself fully into man. Following this, He died a wonderful, all-inclusive death on the cross, and in resurrection man was brought into God. Now divinity is in humanity, and humanity is in divinity. Now a man with all His accomplishments has been brought into the heavens, where He has been glorified and enthroned. The man, Jesus, who is in the heavens, became the very center of all authority. This man who was enthroned, glorified, and anointed, was appointed the Head of the universe, the King of kings, and the Lord of lords. In this way, God and man, divinity and humanity, were brought into one.

On the day of Pentecost, the Holy Spirit came down with all the elements of His divinity, humanity, God being brought into man, man being brought into God, the Lord's human living on earth, and His death, resurrection, ascension, and enthronement. The Holy Spirit with all these elements may be compared to a dose of medicine which is rich and all-inclusive, containing every kind of vitamin and germ-killer; He is the full dose of everything we need. Such a Spirit, who is none other than the Triune God with His many elements and attainments, descended upon the church to authorize and inaugurate the church into its office and function. The coming of the Holy Spirit on the day of Pentecost was the "inauguration ceremony" which brought the church into its office. Now the very Triune God Himself is our life within and our authority without. This means that we are fully one with the Triune God.

THE BAPTISM IN THE HOLY SPIRIT

On the day of Pentecost, the Head, Christ, did not inaugurate many individual believers. Rather, He inaugurated the Body. He baptized the Body into the Holy Spirit (Acts 2:1-4; 1 Cor. 12:13). Therefore, the baptism in the Holy Spirit is a matter of the entire Body.

Being a Fact Accomplished in Two Steps

Moreover, the baptism in the Holy Spirit was accomplished over nineteen hundred years ago. Concerning this matter we must realize that when Christ was crucified on the cross, we were crucified with Him. Also, when Christ was resurrected, we were raised up together with Him (Eph. 2:6a). Even when Christ ascended, we ascended with Him (v. 6b). Not only so, we, the church, were baptized in the Holy Spirit over nineteen hundred years ago.

Acts 1:5 says, "For John baptized with water, but you shall be baptized in the Holy Spirit not many days from now." Verse 8 continues, "But you shall receive power when the Holy Spirit comes upon you." These two verses refer to the same event, but in verse 5 it is called the baptism in the Holy Spirit, while in verse 8 it is called the coming of the Holy Spirit. Since this portion of the word tells us that the Holy Spirit comes upon us, it is outward not inward. This word was fulfilled on the day of Pentecost.

What transpired on the day of Pentecost, however, involved only the Jewish part of the Body. Ephesians 2:15-16 tells us that Christ on the cross created a new man, which is His Body, out of two peoples—the Jews and the Gentiles. This is typified in the Feast of Weeks in the Old Testament (Deut. 16:10). At the fulfillment of the Feast of Weeks, on the day of Pentecost, the children of Israel offered two loaves of bread as a wave offering (Lev. 23:15-17), typifying the two sections of the church, the Jewish part and the Gentile part. On the day of Pentecost the Head, Christ, baptized the Jewish part of the Body into the Holy Spirit. Then the Gentile part of the Body was baptized into the Holy Spirit at Cornelius's house in Acts 10. In 11:15-16 Peter says concerning the house of Cornelius, "And as I began to speak, the Holy Spirit fell on them just as also on us in the beginning. And I remembered the word of the Lord, how He said, John baptized in water, but you shall be baptized in the Holy Spirit." In verse 15, Peter refers to the day of Pentecost, indicating that what happened in the house of Cornelius was also the baptism in the Holy Spirit.

In the New Testament only two cases of the outpouring of the Spirit—the case on the day of Pentecost and the case in the house of Cornelius—are called the baptism in the Holy Spirit (Acts 1:5; 11:15-16). Other than these two, no other cases are spoken of as the baptism in the Holy Spirit. By these two steps, Christ the Head baptized His Body, both the Jewish part on the day of Pentecost and the Gentile part in the house of Cornelius, into the Holy Spirit. Hence, the baptism in the Spirit is an accomplished fact.

Being Experienced
in the Principle of Laying on of Hands

For this reason, the other cases of the outpouring of the Spirit, without exception, required only the laying on of hands. In Acts 8, Peter and John laid hands on the Samaritan believers (v. 17). In the following chapter even Saul of Tarsus did not receive the baptism directly from the Head; he received the experience of the baptism through the laying on of hands by a small disciple, Ananias (9:17). Later, Paul laid hands on the Ephesian believers (19:6).

This indicates that the baptism of the Holy Spirit is already accomplished on the Body, while the experience of the baptism was later obtained by the new members who were added to the Body. The new members needed some older members to represent the Body to bring the new ones into the Body. This identification of the new members with the Body is continuing all the time. Therefore, there is no need for another baptism in the Holy Spirit because the Body has received it already. What we need today is the experience of what the Body has received. The way to experience it is to realize the right relationship with the Body, which is the principle behind the laying on of hands.

The baptism was accomplished by the Head Himself directly on the Body. On the day of Pentecost and in the house of Cornelius the ascended Head directly baptized His Body in the Holy Spirit. However, with all the other cases involving new members being added to the Body, there was the need of an indirect contact through representative members of the Body who laid hands on them to identify them with the Body. The laying on of hands is not a mere form or practice. Rather, it represents the principle of the right relationship with the Body. When we are right with the Body, knit with the Body, and standing with the Body, and when we realize that we are living members of the Body, we receive everything that is of the Body.

In this sense, the laying on of hands can be compared to baptism in water, which also is not a mere form. We need the form of baptism in water, but the form does not accomplish anything in itself; its significance is its principle and reality. In the same way, the laying on of hands is a principle representing the reality of the right relationship with the Body. Ananias, for example, would not have laid hands on a child who was not yet saved. This is because that child had no relationship with the Body. The laying on of hands is based on and represents a relationship with the Body.

The most important matter is that we have a heavenly vision to see what the real significance is of the Lord's resurrection and ascension. Resurrection means that the Triune God—God in Christ as the Spirit—has come into us as our life and nature. By His ascension the Triune God has come down upon us as authority. Therefore, we have the Triune God within as our life and without as our authority. Now, in order for us to experience this authority, this inauguration, we must realize the reality of the Body. We must realize that we are members of the Body, and we must have a proper relationship with the Body. If we are in the Body, with the Body, and for the Body, we are in the position to claim whatever is of the Body.

Thus, it is easy for us to experience the baptism in the Holy Spirit. To experience the baptism is not a matter of speaking in tongues. The experience of the baptism is a matter of authority and power. Many believers have never spoken in tongues, but they do have the authority. This indicates that they have the very experience of the baptism in the Holy Spirit. They have the authority and the power, and they are qualified, equipped, and authorized to do something for the Head in the Body.

Being Different from Our Baptism into Christ

Romans 6:3 and Galatians 3:27 speak of being baptized into Christ. This is different from the baptism in the Holy Spirit. To be baptized into Christ refers to our baptism in water. Although we were born in Adam, through faith and baptism we came out of Adam and into Christ. According to the King James Version, John 3:16 speaks of believing in Christ. However, the Greek preposition here is better translated *into,* as in Romans 6:3, in which Paul tells us that we have been "baptized into Christ Jesus." We believe into Christ and are baptized into Christ. We get into Christ by faith and baptism. The real meaning of water baptism is death and burial. On the positive side, faith indicates that we are one with Christ, while on the negative side, baptism indicates that we are dead to Adam and buried.

We are not saved by baptism in water alone. Salvation by the water of baptism alone is a superstition similar in principle to the teaching of the Catholic Church that the bread and wine of the Lord's table become the actual body and blood of Christ. Rather, baptism by water is a symbol that we are identified with Christ. It is the death and resurrection of Christ implied by the water of baptism that saves us, not the water of baptism in itself.

Thus, there are two kinds of baptism—the baptism with water and the baptism in the Holy Spirit. Baptism by water is a burial, a thorough clearance. The best clearance that we can have is to be buried. After we are buried, all natural relationships, bondage, and other negative matters are terminated. Romans 6:3 and 4 show us the proper meaning of baptism. It is to be buried with Christ.

The baptism in the Holy Spirit, however, is an inauguration, which is something positive. Inauguration is related to power and authority. Although we are identified with Christ by baptism in water, we are not inaugurated by baptism. We were baptized in water as a symbol that we died with Christ and were buried and resurrected with Him, but this is a matter of life not of power or authority. In chapters six, seven, and eight of Romans, there is no mention of the Body of Christ. It is not until we come to chapter twelve that we have the Body. The baptism in the Holy Spirit is a matter of the Body. The Body of Christ as the church was inaugurated by the baptism in the Holy Spirit.

THE WAY TO EXPERIENCE THE TRIUNE GOD WITHIN US AND UPON US

By the resurrection of Christ, the Triune God has come into us as our very life for us to enjoy. Moreover, in His ascension this very Triune God has come down upon the Body of Christ as authority. Now we must experience this full authority by keeping a proper relationship with the Body. We must be right with the Body, stand with the Body, live in the Body, and act in the Body and for the Body. Then we have the ground, the position, to pray and claim whatever has been accomplished on the Body. Now whatever has been accomplished on the Body is our inheritance, our heritage. We simply enjoy it. Christ is our life within and power without.

He is for our inward regeneration and our outward inauguration with authority.

Since the day of Pentecost, there is now a group of persons on the earth who have the Triune God within them as their life and upon them as their authority. They live by this divine life within, and they act, move, and work by this authority without. This group of people is the church, the Body of Christ. If we have this vision, it will be easy to have a living and prevailing faith. Whenever we need power, since we are in the Body and for the Body, we have the position to claim as our portion whatever the Head has accomplished for the Body. We may claim whatever we need for our experience.

Rejecting Ourselves to Live by Christ

We must learn always not to live by ourselves, to reject ourselves, to deny ourselves, because within us is the living One, the Triune God. He was incarnated to be a man and lived on this earth as a man. He passed through human life on the earth and suffered many things. He died on the cross, was resurrected, and as a man was brought into God Himself. This wonderful One today is in us as our life. Therefore, we must learn to live by this living One, not by ourselves or by any teaching or doctrine. What we need is not mere teaching but the real knowledge of a living person, Christ, the Triune God, who lives in us today as our life. We must know how to reject ourselves in order to live by this living One, not according to teaching or regulation but according to the inner anointing.

Acting with Authority in the Body

Then, we must also realize that we are members of the Body, which has been authorized, anointed, and inaugurated by Christ the Head with all His attainments and obtainments. Since we are members of this Body, we can stand in the position of the Body, for the Body, and with the Body for whatever we need. By praying, we can claim for our experience whatever has been accomplished on the Body.

We should not care for what the manifestation of the Spirit upon us will be. Instead, we will simply have authority and power. Then we will not speak things in a vain way with empty words. When we speak, we speak with authority. We will work and do things with authority, not by ourselves but by the One in the heavens. In this sense, we will be like policemen who act with the backing of their government. Those that oppose us will find themselves in trouble, because we do things not by ourselves but by our "uniform," our authority. This is the real significance of the experience of the baptism in the Holy Spirit.

If we are clear about this matter, we will change our way of prayer. We will pray, "Lord, here we are as representatives of Your Body. We are doing things here not on our own but by Your authority. Therefore, You must bring people to us." We must pray in this way and claim by faith. We may compare our bold speaking to that of a policeman; a policeman speaks with authority, and others must obey him. We must exercise the faith that comes from our vision. We see the vision that the Body has been inaugurated with authority on the day of Pentecost, and we are the members of this Body, living and acting in the Body, for the Body, and with the Body. We do not do things by or for ourselves. In this way we have authority and power.

The book of Acts is the record of a group of people who are regenerated by the Triune God and inaugurated with authority by the Triune God. These people have the Triune God within them as their life and upon them as their authority and power. They act in this way and live by the life within. This is the basic thought of the book of Acts. The situation in Christianity today, however, is full of darkness, and there is little impact and authority. The believers mentioned in Acts moved and worked with authority and power, not as many do today.

We must realize the significance of the Lord's resurrection and ascension, including both the breathing of His breath into us on the day of resurrection and the rushing of the violent wind on the day of Pentecost. Now we have the breath within us and the rushing wind upon us. We have the Triune God as our life within and the very same Triune God as our authority without. As such, we are the church. This is the critical transition in the book of Acts.

Praying with Authority in an Aggressive Way

We must stand in the position revealed in the Acts, and we must pray, even with fasting. Many times troubles have come to me, and I have prayed in a simple way, "Lord, You must come in to vindicate the situation. You must come in to interfere." At these times, the Lord did come in. We all can tell the Lord, "Lord, we are not here for ourselves. We are here for You. We are here acting not on our own but as Your Body. You must honor this and do something for Your Body." We need to deal with the Lord in this way. We must be the real Jacobs and not let Him go (Gen. 32:24-26). It is difficult for nice people to fight a battle. In order to fight the battle, we must pray in an aggressive way. Then we will see something happen.

The Triune God is within us as our life and upon us as our authority. If we read the book of Acts again from this point of view we will see this more clearly. This must be our experience. Today this very Jesus, in whom is all that the Triune God has and has obtained, is within us as our life, and this very enthroned One is upon us as our authority. If we live by Him and for Him, we will be different persons, and the church where we are will be different.

CHAPTER EIGHT

THE REAL MEANING OF THE BOOK OF ACTS

Scripture Reading: John 20:22; Matt. 28:18; Psa. 2; Eph. 2:6; Acts 2:1-4; 1:14; 2:14, 46-47; 8:14-17; Rev. 22:1

Many Christians today do not know the real significance of the book of Acts. Although many books have been written about the Acts and many teachings put forth about it, even up to today our understanding of this book may not be very deep. This is because this book records matters that are wonderful and beyond our human concept. We may consider the Acts to be an easy book, relating the story of how the disciples of Christ after His ascension into heaven exercised extraordinary power to do things in a miraculous way, convincing people, bringing people to Christ, and setting up churches. However, if we have only this much understanding of this book, we lack the full revelation and insight.

BEING ENLIVENED BY THE RESURRECTION OF CHRIST

We need the real insight concerning the record of this book. As we saw in the previous chapter, two important things transpired after the Lord's death—resurrection and ascension. Resurrection is the strongest proof that the Son of God is the divine life, a life which nothing can damage, hold, or overcome (Acts 2:24). This life overcomes all things— Satan, death, Hades, and the grave. Nothing and no one can hold Him, damage Him, or overcome Him. This was fully proven and testified by the resurrection of Christ. This is one significance of the resurrection.

However, the resurrection of Christ is not only a proof or testimony; it is also an imparting of Himself into His members. In His resurrection, Christ imparted Himself into all those who identify themselves with Him in faith (1 Pet. 1:3). Therefore, objectively speaking, His resurrection is a proof, a testimony, that He is the indestructible life, and subjectively speaking, it is the imparting of Himself into us to make us the members of His Body.

BEING POSITIONED
IN THE ENTHRONEMENT OF CHRIST

In His ascension, Christ was enthroned and made the very Head over all things in the universe (Eph. 1:22). Therefore, He is the Head, the Lord, the King, and the anointed One on the throne. On the one hand, His ascension was His enthronement. On the other hand, because we were identified with Him in His ascension, we also were brought into the heavens with Him (2:6). When He was crucified, we died in Him on the cross; when He was resurrected, we were raised up with Him; and when He ascended, we also ascended to the heavens with Him. Therefore, His enthronement is our position. Because He is on the throne in the heavens, we also are in the heavens and on the throne. Enthronement indicates authorization. This is why the Lord Jesus told His disciples that all authority in heaven and on earth has been committed to Him (Matt. 28:18). Psalm 2, as a prophecy of Christ's ascension, is the declaration of God to the entire universe that He has enthroned His Son, the anointed One, and made Him the Head over all things.

God committed all authority in the universe to His resurrected and ascended Christ, and now we are in Christ. Therefore, the enthronement of Christ is our position. We are in the heavens on the throne with Christ. The Lord told His disciples to go and disciple all the nations because all authority in heaven and on earth has been given to Him. They were sent not to preach the gospel in a common way but to preach the gospel of the kingdom and make people Christ's disciples. This was carried out not only with His word and His divine life but also with His authority.

By the resurrection of Christ we have been regenerated as His members, and by His ascension we also have been enthroned and brought into the heavens. Resurrection is a matter of life, while ascension is a matter of position. In His resurrection we receive the Triune God within us as our life to be regenerated. In His ascension we have been brought into the heavens to be positioned and enthroned there. These two matters—resurrection and ascension—must be very clear to us. What is the resurrection of Christ? To Christ the resurrection is a proof and testimony that He is the indestructible life, while to us it is the impartation of the Triune God as our life that we might be enlivened and regenerated to become the members of His Body. What is the ascension of Christ? To Christ it is His enthronement, while to us it is our position in the heavenlies on the throne.

EXPERIENCING THE RESURRECTION AND ASCENSION BY THE SPIRIT

How can the wonderful, objective facts accomplished by the resurrection and ascension of Christ be our experience? It is only possible by the experience of the Holy Spirit. It is in the Spirit that all these wonderful facts are applied to us and experienced by us. Without the Spirit, these facts are merely facts and are objective and unrelated to us. Therefore, we need the Spirit.

Regarding the Holy Spirit there are two aspects. On the one hand, the Holy Spirit comes into us as life, while on the other hand, the Spirit comes upon us as power, as authority. Both of these comings have been accomplished. After His resurrection, on "that day" (John 20:19), Christ came to His disciples to breathe Himself into them as the Holy Spirit. When He breathed into the disciples, He said to them, "Receive the Holy Spirit" (v. 22). The Holy Spirit is the very breath of Christ. Our breath which comes out of us is a part of our very being. On the day of resurrection Christ came back to His disciples to breathe Himself into them as the Spirit of life.

The Spirit of life is Christ Himself as the breath of life breathed into the disciples. We should not believe that the Holy Spirit and Christ are separate and have nothing to do with each other. In actuality, these two are one. As we have illustrated before, although water becomes vapor, the water and the vapor are different only in form; in substance they are one. In the same way, Christ is the very Spirit of life which He breathed into the disciples on the day of resurrection.

Following this, Christ ascended to the heavens, and on the day of Pentecost He came down, not to enter into the disciples but to blow upon them as a rushing violent wind (Acts 2:1-4). On the day of resurrection there was the breathing, but on the day of Pentecost there was the rushing of a violent wind. Breathing is for life, while the rushing is for power.

If after Christ resurrected, He did not come back to the disciples on the day of resurrection and breathe into them, what He accomplished by His resurrection would have had nothing to do with the disciples. It was by His breathing that what He accomplished in His resurrection was applied to them. In the same principle, by the blowing of the wind on the day of Pentecost what He accomplished in His ascension was applied to the disciples. By His ascension He was enthroned, and we as His members were also put into the same position, but it was only by the blowing on the day of Pentecost that the enthronement was applied to the disciples.

The day of Pentecost was a day of "inauguration." On election day, a man is voted into the office and position of president, but it is not until the inauguration day that he assumes the real authority as president. We have been put into a heavenly position by the ascension of Christ. However, what was accomplished by His ascension was applied to us on the day of Pentecost when the Spirit came down from the heavens as a rushing violent wind upon the disciples. At that time all the disciples were inaugurated, appointed, with the heavenly power and authority.

APPLYING THE RESURRECTION AND ASCENSION BY FAITH

On the day of resurrection Christ imparted Himself into His disciples as life, while on the day of Pentecost Christ put all of His disciples into Himself. Just as we take water in, Christ dispensed Himself as the living water of life into His disciples on the day of resurrection. Then, just as we baptize people into water, Christ baptized His disciples into Himself on the day of Pentecost. On the day of resurrection Christ put the "water" into the disciples, while on the day of Pentecost He put the disciples into the "water." This water is Christ, the very Triune God. The Triune God was put into us as our life on the day of resurrection, and we were put into the Triune God on the day of Pentecost. The Triune God is power to us; because we have been put into Him, we have been put into His power and authority. Therefore, within us we have the Triune God as our life, and upon us we have the Triune God as our power and authority. We have Christ, the Triune God, as our living drink within and as our clothing and covering without.

All of this has been accomplished and applied to us in Christ's resurrection and ascension. Now all we need to do is to receive it by faith. We should simply take it and say amen. If we would say amen to the Lord, we have it. Christ has resurrected, and on the day of resurrection He applied His resurrection to us. In the same way, the heavenly position and enthronement which Christ obtained in His ascension was applied to us on the day of Pentecost. Even the application of it has been accomplished. Now we need only to say amen to the Lord, and when we say amen, we experience the baptism in the Holy Spirit. The baptism in the Holy Spirit is the application of the enthronement and the heavenly position of Christ.

We must be clear that we were already appointed, inaugurated, and authorized on the day of Pentecost by the ascension of Christ. Because many believers do not have this vision, they are weak, low, and poor. However, if today we do have this vision, we will say, "Amen, Hallelujah! Everything is mine." We will enjoy and experience all these things by faith.

LIVING IN THE ACTS BY DENYING OURSELVES AND LIVING BY THE TRIUNE GOD

The book of Acts is a record of a group of people who are resurrected and ascended with Christ, having Christ within them as their life and Christ upon them as their power and authority. They live not by themselves but by Christ as life.

They forget about their own life and deny themselves. Moreover, they walk, act, and work not by their own strength, their own way, or their own method but by Christ as their power, their way, and their method. This Christ who is now their method, way, and power is the very Holy Spirit who came down upon them. In other words, they live by the Triune God within them as their life, and they act by the Triune God upon them as their strength, their way, and their method. This is the contents of the book of Acts.

If we believe that the resurrection and ascension have been accomplished and applied to us, if we say amen to this and take it by faith, then we must also deny our self all the day long. We must not live by our self but by the Triune God, and we must also forsake all our methods, ways, knowledge, understanding, doctrine, and teachings. We have to abandon all of these things just as those Galilean disciples eventually did. The disciples picked up a great deal of knowledge from Judaism. Peter is a prime example of this. Because Peter was very much influenced by the teachings of Judaism, God was forced to give him a vision from the heavens (Acts 10:9-16). There should have been no need for Peter to have that vision; it was only because he was deeply influenced by the teaching of Judaism.

This is a strong proof that if we want to live in the Acts, we have to drop all the old doctrines. Many of us are still under the wrong influence of the traditional teachings of Christianity. In the record of Acts, the disciples did not act or work according to the teaching of Judaism or according to the Old Testament. All that they did and worked was according to the living guidance of the Triune God who came down after His enthronement to dwell upon them. This group of people lived not by themselves but by Christ within them as their life, and they also walked, worked, and acted not by the old ways, knowledge, or teachings but by the living guidance of the Triune God.

Hence, whenever we live by ourselves we are not in the Acts. Similarly, whenever we work, act, and walk not according to the living guidance of the Triune God but according to regulations, rules, knowledge, and doctrines, we are not a part of the history of the Acts. Instead, we are a part of the history of Christianity. In principle, the Acts is a record only of that group of people who are resurrected and ascended with Christ, having Christ within them as their life and Christ upon them as their power. Moreover, they live not by themselves but by this Christ within, and they act not according to knowledge, doctrine, teaching, rules, regulations, forms, and traditions but according to the living Christ upon them. This is the meaning of the book of Acts. If we take this point of view and go back to read this book again, we will gain the proper insight into it.

PREACHING THE GOSPEL
WITH THE HEAVENLY AUTHORITY

In the Holy Spirit within us we have the reality of resurrection, and with the Holy Spirit upon us we have the reality of ascension. Therefore, within us we have life, and upon us we have authority and power. However, the situation in Christianity today is poor and even pitiful, especially in the preaching of the gospel. Many today use worldly means for the gospel, such as advertising and fund-raising. They do not preach the gospel by the heavenly authority. On the day of Pentecost the disciples preached the gospel not by begging but by the heavenly authorization. In Matthew 28:18-19 Jesus had said, "All authority has been given to Me in heaven and on earth. Go therefore and disciple all the nations." We must go with Christ's authority to preach the gospel. When we go in the name of Jesus to preach the gospel, we have the authority. We should not go as beggars to the worldly people. We must be as ambassadors from heaven to deal with this world. This is the proper way to preach the gospel.

We have Christ's authority as our backing. As His enthronement is ours, we are those coming from the heavens to announce something of our King to His subjects. We speak with authority. This is the right way to preach the gospel. Not only in preaching the gospel, but in any kind of ministering we must stand in the position of Christ's authority. If we look into the Acts thoroughly, we will see a clear picture that all of those sent ones went out with the heavenly power and authority. They had Christ within as their life and Christ without as their authority. Christ became their uniform. Christ is not only our drink but our clothing, our uniform, as well. He is our life and He is our power.

ACTING AND MOVING AS ONE BODY

The entire record of the book of Acts also shows us a group of people who always acted as the Body. From the very first chapter neither Peter, John, nor those one hundred twenty acted individually. Rather, all the actions of this group of people were the actions of the one Body. The one hundred twenty prayed together with one accord, and they received the baptism in the Holy Spirit, preached the gospel, bore the testimony of Jesus, and always moved and acted as one Body (1:14; 2:1, 4, 14, 46-47). From chapter one to chapter twenty-eight, the actions of this group of people were the actions of one Body.

It is difficult to find anyone among them who acted individualistically. Although it appears that Philip preached the gospel by himself in chapter eight when he was in Samaria, it was Peter and John who came to confirm his preaching (vv. 5, 14-17). The Holy Spirit, the power upon the Body, did not come upon those believers through Philip's preaching. It was when Peter and John came and laid hands on the Samaritan believers that the Holy Spirit on the Body was transmitted to them. This proves that even Philip's preaching was not an individual action. His preaching was related to the move of the Body. Therefore, chapter after chapter in the Acts records the move and activity of the Body, not of individual believers.

The activities recorded in Acts were not only of the Body but also for the Body, that is, for the building up of the church. No one acted in a way that had nothing to do with the Body. Rather, every one acted in a way that was for the building up of the Body. The issue and result of what they did was the building up of the church. The activities in this book are absolutely different from the movement of today's Christianity. Many in today's Christianity act in a way that is not of the Body or for the Body. As we have seen, the Acts is a record of a group of people who act and work all the time for the Body and through the Body. Therefore, in this book the churches are built up of out of the activities of those people. The Acts contains a beautiful picture of the one accord in the activities, work, and move of the believers. They always moved in the Body and for the Body.

MOVING, ACTING, AND WORKING IN ONE DIVINE FLOW

Lastly, this book shows us a divine stream, a divine current. This stream flows from the throne in the heavens (Rev. 22:1). What happened in the book of Acts is the same as the picture in Revelation 22. From the throne of God and of Christ, the enthroned Lamb, the flow began, and in the book of Acts it flowed to the earth, beginning from the first station, Jerusalem. All the members of the Body of Christ were in this flow. As this flow proceeded, they simply moved in the current of this flow. This flow eventually went to Antioch (Acts 11:19-21). Antioch became a turning point for the flow to move from the east to the west. From Antioch the flow turned westward across the Aegean Sea, between Asia Minor and Macedonia in the eastern part of Europe, and from that sea the flow reached Europe (16:10-12). From there, the Lord's move went onward to western Europe and Rome (28:14, 30-31). We can draw a line to trace the flow all the way from Jerusalem to Antioch, westward across the sea to eastern Europe, and from there to the middle part of Europe, including Rome.

The divine stream moved westward rather than toward the east. To understand this, we must know the history, geography, and civilization of the time. At that time it was difficult for people to go eastward. There was no way to turn but toward the west. History tells us that the Roman Empire built many highways. Moreover, there was much traffic on the Mediterranean Sea, and it was very easy for people to sail from Palestine to the west. Not only so, there was much intermingling of the people, and their language and even citizenship were brought together. There was no need to obtain a permit to travel. As long as someone was a Roman citizen, he could travel throughout the entire Mediterranean area. In this way, all the different countries became one under the Roman Empire.

Beginning from Jerusalem in Acts 2 there was only one flow on this earth, and all the early disciples moved, acted, and worked in the flow. There were not two currents in the flow, but always one. All those who were raised up by the Lord sooner or later were brought into the flow. While the flow proceeded westward, believers such as Aquila, Priscilla, Apollos, and others were raised up by the Lord and brought into this one stream (18:2, 24-28).

There is no record of more than one stream. Barnabas was in this one flow up to a certain point; after that he was separated from the flow (15:35-39). Following this, there is no further record of Barnabas in the book of Acts, because he was no longer in the flow. There was only one stream, one current, of the flow. The flow was not like today's turnpikes, which branch in every direction and confuse people. In the New Jerusalem there is only one flow, one way.

Today there are many works which are not in the one flow, as exemplified by the work of Barnabas. The work of Barnabas was not in the flow, whereas the work of the apostle Paul and his co-workers was. We may do a work for the Lord, yet our work may not be in the one divine flow. Throughout the entire history of the church there has always been a situation that some of the Christian work was in this unique flow, but many works were not in the flow, even though these works were for the Lord. The work of Roman Catholicism, for example, is a work for the Lord, but it is not in the one flow. The work in the flow is the work of the Lord's present testimony.

Thus far we have seen the principles of the book of Acts. If we apply these principles when we read chapter after chapter, we will be clear about what is in the Acts. We will know its real meaning, and we will have the insight into it. The central meaning of the flow in the Acts is that there is a group of people who know the meaning of resurrection and ascension. They live not by themselves but by Christ as their life, and they act not according to certain ways or methods but by the living Christ as their strength, power, method, and way. Moreover, they realize that they are the Body, and they always act in the Body and for the Body in the one divine stream. May we all be clear to such an extent that we not only know the resurrection and ascension, but we live in resurrection and act in ascension, not by ourselves but in the Body, for the Body, and in one flow. This is the real meaning of the book of Acts.

ABOUT THE AUTHOR

Witness Lee was born in 1905 in northern China and raised in a Christian family. At age 19 he was fully captured for Christ and immediately consecrated himself to preach the gospel for the rest of his life. Early in his service, he met Watchman Nee, a renowned preacher, teacher, and writer. Witness Lee labored together with Watchman Nee under his direction. In 1934 Watchman Nee entrusted Witness Lee with the responsibility for his publication operation, called the Shanghai Gospel Bookroom.

Prior to the Communist takeover in 1949, Witness Lee was sent by Watchman Nee and his other co-workers to Taiwan to ensure that the things delivered to them by the Lord would not be lost. Watchman Nee instructed Witness Lee to continue the former's publishing operation abroad as the Taiwan Gospel Bookroom, which has been publicly recognized as the publisher of Watchman Nee's works outside China. Witness Lee's work in Taiwan manifested the Lord's abundant blessing. From a mere 350 believers, newly fled from the mainland, the churches in Taiwan grew to 20,000 in five years.

In 1962 Witness Lee felt led of the Lord to come to the United States, settling in California. During his 35 years of service in the U.S., he ministered in weekly meetings and weekend conferences, delivering several thousand spoken messages. Much of his speaking has since been published as over 400 titles. Many of these have been translated into over fourteen languages. He gave his last public conference in February 1997 at the age of 91.

He leaves behind a prolific presentation of the truth in the Bible. His major work, *Life-study of the Bible,* comprises over 25,000 pages of commentary on every book of the Bible from the perspective of the believers' enjoyment and experience of God's divine life in Christ through the Holy Spirit. Witness Lee was the chief editor of a new translation of the New Testament into Chinese called the Recovery Version and directed the translation of the same into English. The Recovery Version also appears in a number of other languages. He provided an extensive body of footnotes, outlines, and spiritual cross references. A radio broadcast of his messages can be heard on Christian radio stations in the United States. In 1965 Witness Lee founded Living Stream Ministry, a non-profit corporation, located in Anaheim, California, which officially presents his and Watchman Nee's ministry.

Witness Lee's ministry emphasizes the experience of Christ as life and the practical oneness of the believers as the Body of Christ. Stressing the importance of attending to both these matters, he led the churches under his care to grow in Christian life and function. He was unbending in his conviction that God's goal is not narrow sectarianism but the Body of Christ. In time, believers began to meet simply as the church in their localities in response to this conviction. In recent years a number of new churches have been raised up in Russia and in many eastern European countries.

OTHER BOOKS PUBLISHED BY
Living Stream Ministry

Titles by Witness Lee:

Abraham—Called by God	0-7363-0359-6
The Experience of Life	0-87083-417-7
The Knowledge of Life	0-87083-419-3
The Tree of Life	0-87083-300-6
The Economy of God	0-87083-415-0
The Divine Economy	0-87083-268-9
God's New Testament Economy	0-87083-199-2
The World Situation and God's Move	0-87083-092-9
Christ vs. Religion	0-87083-010-4
The All-inclusive Christ	0-87083-020-1
Gospel Outlines	0-87083-039-2
Character	0-87083-322-7
The Secret of Experiencing Christ	0-87083-227-2
The Life and Way for the Practice of the Church Life	0-87083-785-0
The Basic Revelation in the Holy Scriptures	0-87083-105-4
The Crucial Revelation of Life in the Scriptures	0-87083-372-3
The Spirit with Our Spirit	0-87083-798-2
Christ as the Reality	0-87083-047-3
The Central Line of the Divine Revelation	0-87083-960-8
The Full Knowledge of the Word of God	0-87083-289-1
Watchman Nee—A Seer of the Divine Revelation ...	0-87083-625-0

Titles by Watchman Nee:

How to Study the Bible	0-7363-0407-X
God's Overcomers	0-7363-0433-9
The New Covenant	0-7363-0088-0
The Spiritual Man 3 volumes	0-7363-0269-7
Authority and Submission	0-7363-0185-2
The Overcoming Life	1-57593-817-0
The Glorious Church	0-87083-745-1
The Prayer Ministry of the Church	0-87083-860-1
The Breaking of the Outer Man and the Release ...	1-57593-955-X
The Mystery of Christ	1-57593-954-1
The God of Abraham, Isaac, and Jacob	0-87083-932-2
The Song of Songs	0-87083-872-5
The Gospel of God 2 volumes	1-57593-953-3
The Normal Christian Church Life	0-87083-027-9
The Character of the Lord's Worker	1-57593-322-5
The Normal Christian Faith	0-87083-748-6
Watchman Nee's Testimony	0-87083-051-1

Available at
Christian bookstores, or contact Living Stream Ministry
2431 W. La Palma Ave. • Anaheim, CA 92801
1-800-549-5164   • www.livingstream.com